The Christian's True Identity

The Christian's True Identity

What It Means to Be in Christ

JONATHAN LANDRY CRUSE

Reformation Heritage Books
Grand Rapids, Michigan

The Christian's True Identity
© 2019 by Jonathan Landry Cruse

Reformation Heritage Books
3070 29th St. SE
Grand Rapids, MI 49512
616-977-0889
orders@heritagebooks.org
www.heritagebooks.org

Scripture taken from the New King James Version®. Copyright © 1982 by Thomas Nelson. Used by permission. All rights reserved.

All emphases in Scripture quotations have been added by the author.

Printed in the United States of America
22 23 24 25 26/10 9 8 7 6 5 4 3 2

Library of Congress Cataloging-in-Publication Data

Names: Cruse, Jonathan Landry, author.
Title: The Christian's true identity : what it means to be in Christ / Jonathan Landry Cruse.
Description: Grand Rapids : Reformation Heritage Books, 2019. | Includes bibliographical references. | Summary: "An introduction to the Christian doctrine of union with Christ and the benefits of being united to Christ"—Provided by publisher.
Identifiers: LCCN 2019031457 (print) | LCCN 2019031458 (ebook) | ISBN 9781601787255 (paperback) | ISBN 9781601787262 (epub)
Subjects: LCSH: Mystical union.
Classification: LCC BT767.7 .C78 2019 (print) | LCC BT767.7 (ebook) | DDC 233—dc23
LC record available at https://lccn.loc.gov/2019031457
LC ebook record available at https://lccn.loc.gov/2019031458

For additional Reformed literature, request a free book list from Reformation Heritage Books at the above regular or email address.

"While many books have been written on the doctrine of the believer's union with Christ, there is still a need for a text that can give a clear explanation of this comforting truth and its benefits to the average reader. That is, until now. With *The Christian's True Identity*, Jonathan Cruse has filled this need, drawing from his experience as poet and preacher to communicate the beauty and magnitude of this doctrine in a clear, direct, and heartening manner."

—Simonetta Carr, author of *Broken Pieces and the God Who Mends Them* and Christian Biographies for Young Readers

"Jonathan Cruse offers a rich and accessible account of the believer's union with Christ, a vital biblical teaching. Forged on the anvil of Scripture and the day-to-day challenges of the Christian life, Pastor Cruse points readers to life-giving truth in very practical and real ways. This book will help people in the pews gain a greater knowledge of how God has united them to Christ, from their election to their glorification."

—J. V. Fesko, professor of systematic and historical theology, Reformed Theological Seminary, Jackson, Mississippi

"Reading Jonathan Cruse's volume on *The Christian's True Identity* is like enjoying a finely crafted meal; the various ingredients are so properly proportioned to one another that one hardly notices the numerous details because they are so harmoniously blended. There is not only a surprising amount of truth in this slender volume, but there is an enormous amount of important, Christ-centered truth, an enormous amount of gospel, presented in a manner that is responsive to twenty-first-century concerns without being swallowed by them. Readers will be saddened when they arrive at the end of this pithy volume."

—T. David Gordon, professor of religion and Greek, Grove City College, Grove City, Pennsylvania

"With winsome warmth and refreshing clarity, Pastor Jonathan Cruse shows us how infinitely better it is to have *God* define our identity—in Christ—rather than trying to invent and reinvent ourselves! Instead of pandering to our self-esteem, this little book speaks straight, sobering truth about our guilt and brokenness. But it also directs our hearts to an astonishing reality: God removes our shame and robes us in Jesus's beauty, embracing us in grace. God's answer to our question Who am I? gives rest to our restless hearts and replaces aimless ennui with life-energizing purpose."

—Dennis E. Johnson, professor emeritus of practical theology,
Westminster Seminary California

"Dear believer—in what or in whom do you find your true identity? This is a question that every Christian should be able to answer with relative ease. And yet in our age of superficial evangelicalism, it seems that few believers are equipped to do so. In *The Christian's True Identity*, Jonathan Landry Cruse beautifully and skillfully unpacks the riches of the gospel, powerfully demonstrating how union with Christ—and the benefits that flow from that union—define and shape the believer's true identity. Spiritually united to Christ and fully accepted in the beloved, we no longer let the world define us or press us into its idolatrous mold. Now that's good news that fosters both freedom and piety! Read and digest this book. You will never be the same."

—Jon D. Payne, senior pastor, Christ Church Presbyterian,
Charleston, South Carolina and executive coordinator,
Gospel Reformation Network

"When you forget who you are in Christ, you quit seeking and celebrating what belongs to you in Christ. This book is a welcome cure for the identity amnesia that wreaks havoc on the lives of many Christians and weakens the mission of the church. Read it carefully and then go live its message with hope, courage, and joy."

—Paul Tripp, author of *Instruments in the Redeemer's Hands*

For Kerri Ann,
my one in Christ

CONTENTS

ACKNOWLEDGMENTS

I wish to thank, at the outset, the whole host of friends and colleagues who helped make this book a reality. A number of people graciously read portions of this manuscript or the whole thing and offered helpful feedback and critique. John Fesko and Dennis Johnson were particularly encouraging during this process. Additionally, Aimee Byrd, Simonetta Carr, Drew Cruse (my dad), Bob Jackson, Michelle Reed, and Perry Westerman are to be acknowledged: their comments and suggestions have made this a much stronger work, and any remaining shortcomings are my own.

I am extremely grateful for the team at RHB (Joel Beeke, Jay Collier, David Woollin, Annette Gysen, and many others!) for supporting this work, and for their labors to get the manuscript published. They have been an absolute pleasure to work with.

Special thanks is due to the saints of Community Presbyterian Church in Kalamazoo, Michigan, who dutifully and eagerly sit under the preaching of God's Word every week. They first heard this material as it was presented in sermonic form during the summer of 2018 and were then, and continue to be, a great encouragement to this pastor.

Finally, I want to thank my wife, Kerri Ann. She is truly my partner and support through all the ups and downs of life and ministry. It was with her I first mulled over the idea of this project, and it is with her that I continue to seek to live out the reality of being in Christ. No one is more faithful at reminding me of my identity in Christ than she is. For that, I am forever grateful.

UNION *with* HIM

*To them God willed to make known what are the riches
of the glory of this mystery among the Gentiles: which
is Christ in you, the hope of glory.*

—COLOSSIANS 1:27

Who am I?

What is your initial reaction to that question? You are
the person you spend the most time with and think of most
often, but can you define yourself? In actuality, we are defin-
ing ourselves all the time through the decisions we make
and the actions we take, in the ways we spend our time and
the people we choose to spend it with, and by what we consider to be most meaningful and fulfilling in life. These are
the ways in which we implicitly answer the question, Who
am I? But now let's make it explicit. Let's bring it out from
the recesses of our hearts and minds and shed some light
on it. How would you answer? What gets to the core of who
you are as an individual? What makes you "you"?

Some of us may answer it in terms of our relation to
others: I am a parent; I am a spouse; I am an employer.

We might answer it based on personality: I am funny; I am slightly neurotic; I am uptight. Many of us likely think of our careers immediately when we hear the question: I am a lawyer; I am a dental hygienist; I am a freelance photographer; I am an administrative assistant; I am a dishwasher at the local diner; I am an Uber driver on the weekends. Maybe we think of our hobbies: I am a cyclist; I am a woodworker; I am a seamstress. We might answer it based on personal background: I am a Jones; I am a Canadian. Maybe we think of certain groups we affiliate with: I am a feminist; I am a Republican; I am a PETA activist. The answer might be influenced by our achievements in life: I am an award-winning author; I am a championship athlete; I am a celebrated musician. Other people's first thought might be their lack of achievements or perceived failures and shortfalls in life: I am twice divorced; I am unattractive; I am overweight; I am awkward, unpopular, and have few friends; I am a nobody.

What first came to your mind? Our initial reaction to that question reveals something deeply personal about us, whether we like it or not. It tells us what we think is the controlling aspect of our existence, what the purpose of our lives is—even if it is something we might not express openly or share with others. Ultimately, the answer to this question reveals what we believe is our identity.

The Sacred Self

In 2015, after years-long cultural debate, the Supreme Court case *Obergefell v. Hodges* spoke the definitive word on legally constituting same-sex marital unions in the United States. Interestingly, Justice Anthony Kennedy opened his majority report in terms that spoke about more than just gay rights with a statement indicative of the spirit and ethos of our modern age: "The Constitution promises liberty to all within its reach, a liberty that includes certain specific rights that allow persons, within a lawful realm, to define and express their identity."[1] In essence, Kennedy was echoing himself from another opinion years earlier: "At the heart of liberty is the right to define one's own concept of existence."[2]

With these words Justice Kennedy had codified the thought of today's average American: there is nothing more important than answering that question, Who am I? We are taught (indoctrinated perhaps?) to believe that all things are meant to serve our attempt to discover and live out our identity. The ultimate object of life is to find satisfaction and fulfillment in our self-expression.

Hence, in recent years societies around the globe have become increasingly individualistic. We live in the age of "selfies" and a "you-do-you" mentality—a time when *identity* was recently voted word of the year.[3] A person's identity, or their particular mode of self-expression, is sacred in our

---

1. *Obergefell v. Hodges*, 135 S. Ct. 2584 (2015), Justia (website), https://supreme.justia.com/cases/federald/us/576/14–556/.

2. *Planned Parenthood of Southeastern Pa. v. Casey*, 505 U. S. 833, 851 (1992), Cornell University Law School Legal Information Institute, https://www.law.cornell.edu/wex/quotation/[field_short_title-raw]_25.

3. Katy Steinmetz, "This Is Dictionary.com's 2015 Word of the Year," *Time*, December 8, 2015, http://time.com/4139350/dictionary-2015-word -of-the-year/.

current context. There is nothing more important, our society says, than allowing people to identify themselves in whatever way they see fit.

The Identity Gospel

This is not just the world's problem—the church is not immune to promoting this kind of ideology either. Why talk about sin when people feel much more comfortable being told God wants them to be happy being themselves? The false "health, wealth, prosperity gospel" of the past several decades is giving way to what we might call a false "identity gospel." This false gospel teaches that God simply wants you to be content with who you are—in your social circles, in your sexuality, in your gender expression, in whatever. As long as you are being "true to yourself," you are being true to God. As long as you are "following your heart," you are following God. Scripture gets twisted or tossed out to ensure that people feel no pressure to conform to any kind of moral norm—they are free to set their own course. So this false gospel preaches that man's chief end is to glorify *himself* and enjoy *himself* forever.

How fascinating it is, then, to compare this trend of the twenty-first century, and in particular Justice Kennedy's words that "at the heart of liberty is the right to define one's own concept of existence" with the opening of the 1563 Heidelberg Catechism. The first question asks, "What is your only comfort in life and in death?" The answer? "*That I am not my own.*"

Isn't that astounding? This catechism was a theological document commissioned by the ruler of a German province and would go on to be learned and loved by many European Christians for centuries to come. Yet it couldn't be further from the prevailing mind-set of today. What was seen as freeing back then is viewed as being in exact opposition to the heart of liberty today. If the catechism were to be rewritten now, it might go something like this: "What is your only comfort in life and in death—that is, what keeps you motivated, inspired, and going every day?" Answer: "That I *am* my own and can be whatever and whoever *I* want to be, and *no one* can stop me."

While that does sound inspirational and empowering, where has this false identity gospel led us? It has led to people finding their identity in things like family, gender, race, sexuality, nationality, grades, or careers. These are things that are not wrong in and of themselves but when given such ultimate prominence in our lives, the result has been disastrous. It has led to numerous controversies that split party lines and family ties. It has led to bitter resentment and hatred toward others and deep dissatisfaction and disappointment with ourselves.

It is no wonder the repercussions can be so grave, since these are really important matters. After all, we are talking about what makes us who we are. Of course that is a crucial question—and wouldn't it be a terrible one to get wrong?

The Problem

But that is the problem. Countless people today are finding their identity in the wrong thing. They are answering that question of who they are in the wrong way. An identity that is based on relationships, job performance, or circumstances will always come up short of giving us the satisfaction we are after. It might feel good for a while—and many can attest that it *does* feel good—but it will never last. The happiness that these identities offer is always fleeting and fading. Why?

As Timothy Keller explains, "To have an identity is to have something sustained that is true of you in every setting. Otherwise there would be no 'you.'"[4] So the hunt for an identity is the hunt for something that is true of me in every circumstance I am in. But we are illusory, changing beings. Our desires are constantly in flux. If we try to base our identity on any of these aforementioned transient things, we will find ourselves constantly disoriented, lost, and unfulfilled. The identity gospel falls short of giving what it promises.

Furthermore, while the quest for self-expression is often billed as being inherently freeing, in reality it proves itself to be mercilessly demanding and oppressive. In *The Weariness of Self*, Dr. Alain Ehrenberg explains why depression has become the most diagnosed mental disorder in the world: because of increased feelings of inadequacy. That is, there is an unrealistic expectation of the individual to be successful and satisfied, and anytime that is unmet (which is always), people are prone to spiral into despair.[5] To state it simply: we put too much pressure on temporary things to give us lasting, eternal satisfaction.

---

4. Timothy Keller, *Making Sense of God* (New York: Penguin, 2016), 118.

5. As quoted in Rankin Wilbourne, *Union with Christ* (Colorado Springs: David C. Cook, 2016), 139.

There is a story in the New Testament that teaches this tragic point: the parable of the rich man and Lazarus (Luke 16:19–31). What is interesting about this parable is that it is the only one in which Jesus gives one of the characters a name. The significance may be in further distinguishing these men in the afterlife. The former, who strove his whole life to make a name for himself with riches and renown, has nothing to comfort him while he is tormented in hell, and he remains anonymous. He is simply "the rich man." But the latter has an identity. He has a name by which even God in heaven knows him—a name, incidentally, which means "God has helped."[6]

The parable reveals to us that we are dealing with an age-old problem. Humanity has spent and will continue to spend everything in pursuit of satisfaction, in pursuit of a name, in pursuit of recognition, in pursuit of happiness. We will spend everything and gain nothing. We will search our whole lives for an identity, only to end up anonymous and unknown. "For what will it profit a man if he gains the whole world, and loses his own soul?" (Mark 8:36).

Union with Christ

If that is the problem, then what is the solution? Let's return to the insights of that ancient catechism from Germany: "What is your only comfort in life and in death? That I am not my own, *but belong body and soul, both in life and in death, to my faithful savior Jesus Christ*" (emphasis added). According to the Heidelberg Catechism, our hope, secu-

---

6. See Leon Morris, *Luke* (Grand Rapids: Eerdmans, 1988), 276.

rity, fulfillment, and satisfaction in this life can never come from us. They come from disowning ourselves and finding our all in Jesus Christ. It is not by being an unnamed rich man, but by being a person whose help is God alone. This is a radical message to hear today, but it is a freeing message. It is a life-giving message.

For the Christian, our identity is not something we earn, but something we are given. It is not something we find inside of ourselves; it is something that is intrinsically outside of ourselves in the person of Jesus Christ. He becomes our identity. The Bible is exceedingly clear on this point. Scripture sums up this profoundly important concept in just two little words: "in Him." In other words, everything that we have and everything that we are is found *in* the person of Jesus Christ.

The technical term for this concept is *union with Christ*. It is a doctrine you may or may not have heard of before, but you have certainly read about it if you have ever skimmed through the New Testament. We never come across the phrase "union with Christ" in Scripture, but we encounter phrases like "in Him," "in Christ," and "in the Lord," among others. These are favorites of the apostle Paul in particular. Once you start looking for it, you will be amazed by just how often the phrase "in Him" or one of its variations appears in the New Testament. You won't be able to miss it! According to one trusted scholar, there are no fewer than 160 mentions of believers being in Christ.[7]

---

7. See Bruce Demarest, T*he Cross and Salvation: The Doctrine of Salvation* (Wheaton, Ill.: Crossway, 1993), 80–81.

The numbers should speak for themselves; this is an important doctrine. See what John Murray, longtime professor at Westminster Theological Seminary, had to say about the doctrine: "Nothing is more central or basic than union and communion with Christ. Union with Christ is really *the central truth of the whole doctrine of salvation* not only in its application but also in its once-for-all accomplishment in the finished work of Christ."[8]

Murray was not alone in his estimation of this doctrine. Seventeenth-century theologian John Owen referred to union with Christ as the "measure of all spiritual enjoyments and expectations."[9] Puritan Thomas Goodwin writes that "being in Christ, and united to him, is the fundamental constitution of a Christian."[10] Reformer John Calvin said the doctrine deserves "the highest degree of importance."[11] What these men understood was that the biblical evidence was relentless in impressing on us the centrality of this truth. That is, there is something here we need to grasp if we are to fully understand the riches and reach of our salvation in Christ. And I would like to put it this way: union

---

8. John Murray, *Redemption Accomplished and Applied* (1955; repr., Grand Rapids: Eerdmans, 2015), 161 (emphasis added).

9. As quoted in Joel R. Beeke and Mark Jones, *A Puritan Theology: Doctrine for Life* (Grand Rapids: Reformation Heritage Books, 2012), 483.

10. Thomas Goodwin, *Of Christ the Mediator, in The Works of Thomas Goodwin*, ed. Thomas Smith (1861–1866; repr., Grand Rapids: Reformation Heritage Books, 2006), 5:350.

11. John Calvin, *Institutes of the Christian Religion,* trans. Ford Lewis Battles (Philadelphia: Westminster Press, 1960), 3.11.10.

with Christ teaches us that salvation is not something we *get* from Jesus; salvation *is* Jesus.

Perhaps that seems overly simplistic, but for many believers it is a groundbreaking concept. Many of us are raised believing that Jesus is simply the *way* to salvation. But no—He *is* salvation. He is the way, but He is also the life! He is both the giver *and* the gift. He is not a means to an end; He is the end. We are not to come to Christ looking for Him to give us *something* (like salvation, sanctification, a better life—or at least a better car), but instead we are to come to Christ looking for Him. And when we receive Him, we receive everything we need. A great issue with many Christians is that we flee to Christ seeking something from Him other than Himself. Yet it is no small consolation to know that our Lord is so gracious that even when we come with other motives, He welcomes us anyway. Then His Spirit enables us, slowly but surely, to discover over time that our deepest thirst was ultimately not for His gifts but for Him.

So what this beautiful doctrine unashamedly teaches us is that Christ is truly *all* (Eph. 1:23). And when we are in Him, we have "all things" as well (Rom. 8:32; cf. 1 Cor. 3:22). Apart from Jesus we are nothing and we have nothing. But in Christ we are filled with the very fullness of God (Col. 2:9)—God "has blessed us with every spiritual blessing in the heavenly places *in Christ*" (Eph. 1:3). This doctrine ought to magnify our love for Christ, our desire for Him, and our adoration and praise for Him. This doctrine ought to move us to say with the apostle Paul that we have no greater desire than to know Christ and be "found in Him" (Phil. 3:9; see vv. 7–11).

What Union Is and Is Not

To be clear, union with Christ does not mean we become Christ. It is not a form of deification where we slowly turn into gods or become one with the divine essence. This is mysticism, not the Christian religion. Nor are we literally or physically united to Him, as though we become conjoined twins attached at the hip. The biblical conception of union is manifold, but it ultimately comes down to this: it is a *spiritual* union, a work wrought through the power of the Holy Spirit.

After all, Jesus is now ascended and sitting at the right hand of the Father in heaven. We are not in heaven, so how could it be said that we are united to Him? It must be through a mysterious working of the Spirit. By faith, the Holy Spirit brings us into a union with Jesus that is personal, real, vital (life-giving), and unbreakable—a union that can span even the distance between heaven and earth. John Owen explains how the whole of union hangs on the work of the Spirit of Christ when he says, "Two men cannot be one, because they have two souls; no more could we be one with Christ were it not the same Spirit in him and us."[12] It is the Holy Spirit who enables us to be one with Christ.

It should also be noted that our union with Christ doesn't erase our individuality. Take John and Paul (the

---

12. John Owen, *The Duty of Pastors and People Distinguished, in The Works of John Owen*, ed. William H. Goold (Edinburgh: T&T Clark, n.d.), 13:22.

apostles, not the musicians), for example. These two men understood the importance of union with Christ—and were both united to Christ—and yet they each had different callings, personalities, and styles of writing. Even when teaching about this doctrine, John preferred the poetic imagery of "abiding" in Christ like a branch that grows and produces fruit from a vine (John 15), whereas Paul by and large stuck with the punchy, staccato "in Him" language. So union with Christ does not make us boringly homogeneous and the same (more on that in chapter 6). What union with Christ does is takes us individually—with our own interests, hobbies, senses of humor, quirks, and all—and brings us into a saving relationship with the one Christ.

Furthermore, the doctrine of union does not render those things we often identify ourselves by—family, career, gender, sexuality—unimportant or meaningless. Far from it. Rather, our identity in Christ is a fundamental identity that claims every other identity that we could possibly have. Put another way, our identity in Christ is the lens through which every other identity becomes accountable. J. Todd Billings writes that "no part of human identity goes untouched by union with Christ."[13]

Hence, the issue is not having a "gender identity" per se; the issue is having a gender identity that the Lord does not recognize as virtuous. Similarly, the issue would be owning a sexual identity that does not conform to the will of Christ. The problem is not having a career; the problem

---

13. J. Todd Billings, *Union with Christ: Reframing Theology and Ministry for the Church* (Grand Rapids: Baker Academic, 2011), 11.

is making a career your crutch to get through life. Parenthood is a wonderful blessing and calling, but "mom" or "dad" is never meant to be who we are in an ultimate sense. To have an identity that is rooted in Christ will claim, cleanse, and control all other aspects of who we are. An identity in Christ will give renewed meaning, invigorating purpose, and God-glorifying direction to everything else we do in life.

The Hope of Glory

Though the New Testament, and in particular the writings of Paul, is overflowing with language of our being *in* Christ, we also find the reverse in Scripture: that Christ is *in* us. Union is, indeed, a two-way street. Perhaps this is better conveyed by using the word *communion*. In the Greek that would be the word *koinonia*, which can also be translated as "fellowship" or "sharing." There is reciprocity between Christ and His people. Dutch theologian Wilhelmus à Brakel puts it this way: "All true believers are the property of Christ, and Christ is the property of all true believers."[14] Or, as we sing some Sundays, "I am His, and He is mine."[15]

What does this mean? It means that everything that is Christ's is rightfully ours, and everything that is ours is rightfully Christ's. We receive His sinlessness, righteousness, inheritance, glory, and much more. He receives our sin, wretchedness, filth, weakness, poverty, judgment, and

---

14. Wilhelmus à Brakel, *The Christian's Reasonable Service* (1700; repr., Ligonier, Pa.: Soli Deo Gloria, 1993), 2:87.

15. George Wade Robinson, "Loved with Everlasting Love" (1890), in the public domain.

curse. It is by no means a fair and equal trade. Yet this is the infinite love that God has toward His chosen people in Christ Jesus: "For He made Him who knew no sin to be sin for us, that we might become the righteousness of God in Him" (2 Cor. 5:21).

So it is just as important to recognize that while we are in Christ, He is in us as well. He is in us, by His incarnation. Through the incarnation, Jesus truly knows us, knows our frame and frailty, knows our weaknesses and temptations. Theologian Robert Letham writes that "we can become one with him because he first became one with us. By taking human nature into personal union, the Son of God has joined himself to humanity. He now has a human body and soul, which he will never jettison."[16]

But even more astounding than that is the reality that Christ is *literally* in us through the powerful working of the Spirit: "By this we know that we abide in Him, and He in us, because He has given us of His Spirit" (1 John 4:13). In Colossians 1:27, Paul bursts forth into praise and doxology when he declares, "Christ *in* you [is] the hope of glory." Our eternal peace, hope, and joy rest on the fact that not only are we found in Christ but He has graciously condescended to be found in us poor, miserable sinners.

But apart from this union and communion with Christ, we can have no claim to the hope of heaven. We can have no access to the glories of Christ. Apart from being in Him, we cannot share in His saving benefits. But the very

---

16. Robert Letham, *Union with Christ: In Scripture, History, and Theology* (Phillipsburg, N.J.: P&R, 2011), 21.

instant we put our faith in Jesus Christ, the Spirit draws us into Christ and Christ into us and we have every spiritual blessing. Do you see how much richer and fuller your life is once you have Christ and are united to Him?

Conclusion

So who are you? What gets to the core of you as an individual? What makes you "you"? What is that one thing that is true of you in every circumstance of life?

In this book, I hope to show you that everything you need for a lasting, fulfilling identity is found in Christ—and only in Christ. I hope to dissuade you of buying into this false "identity gospel" that is becoming so prevalent in the culture and the church. I hope to show you Christ as your all in all. I want you to echo Paul's desire to be found in Christ. My prayer for you is that your immediate, heart-felt answer to the question, Who am I? is, "I am a Christian! I am in Christ!"

To that end, each of the following chapters will take a passage from one of Paul's epistles and show how those tiny words "in Him" make a big difference—an eternal difference. For in Him we are chosen and loved, redeemed and forgiven, cleansed and made new. In Him we are kept secure and made truly alive. This is the Christian's true identity. It is an identity that the world cannot offer and with which the world cannot compete. Nothing but an identity founded in Christ is sustainable through all the changes of life and will satisfy even into eternity.

Are you found in Him?

Questions for Further Study

1. What first comes to mind when you ask yourself the question, Who am I?

2. In what ways does our culture view identity or personal self-expression as sacred?

3. In your own words, how would you define the doctrine of union with Christ?

4. Why is this doctrine so important?

5. What does union with Christ have to do with the concept of identity?

CHOSEN *in* HIM

Blessed be the God and Father of our Lord Jesus Christ, who has blessed us with every spiritual blessing in the heavenly places in Christ, just as He chose us in Him before the foundation of the world, that we should be holy and without blame before Him in love, having predestined us to adoption as sons by Jesus Christ to Himself, according to the good pleasure of His will, to the praise of the glory of His grace, by which He made us accepted in the Beloved.
—EPHESIANS 1:3–6

We are faced with countless choices in our lives. On a daily basis, we choose what kind of outfit we are going to wear, what we are going to eat for the day, which line to get in at the grocery store, what route to take to work. Weightier choices present themselves at more significant moments: Where will we attend school? What career path will we take? Whom will we marry? The weightiness of a choice is also dependent on your particular circumstance: for an eight-year-old team captain on the playground, choosing which teammates he wants on his dodgeball team seems to be just as critical of a proposition as a presidential candidate choosing his or her running mate.

But in any scenario, there is one basic principle that remains the same. It is a principle that is at play any and every time we make a decision, choosing one thing over something (or somethings) else. It might seem overly simplistic and obvious, but I'll state it anyway: we choose what we think is best. We don't wake up in the morning and intentionally put on a clashing outfit or eat food we hate or pick the longest line at the grocery store or take the slow route to work. We choose schools that we think will challenge us and help us develop into specialists in our respective fields. We choose jobs based on availability, salary and benefit packages, family obligations, and geographical restrictions. Which is the best option with all these considerations? And I am man enough (now) to admit that I was always picked last for dodgeball because the other kids knew I had bad aim and was an easy target—I was clearly not the best option.

From the time we are old enough to make decisions, we base them on what seems best, feels best, or is objectively best. At the market, why do we check the produce instead of just throwing it into the cart? We examine the fruit to make sure we are purchasing the best that is available. We want to walk away with a bag of ripe apples, not bruised ones. We choose what is best. So why did God choose me?

It takes some honest self-reflection and humility, but that is the question, is it not? If the pervading principle of making a good choice is choosing good things, then why would God choose me? I'm far from the best. I'm not even good. If we return to the market analogy, I'm not the ripe fruit fresh from the farm. I'm the moldy, rotten, shriveled, and petrified apple carcass that was delivered months ago and stayed stuck at the bottom of the barrel. Martin Luther said it best: "The truth is, I am all sin."[1] Why would God want someone like that?

That is one of the first questions many people as new believers must wrestle with. But the dilemma doesn't disappear the longer you are a Christian. The reality remains the same: we are awful, wretched, and weak sinners. We have done things we wish we could forget, things we are ashamed to own up to. We can at times feel physically repulsed by our spiritual shortcomings. And so it would be understandable if we returned to this question over and over: Why me? Why would God choose me? The answer to that question is found in the doctrine of our union with Christ.

He Chose
Before we get to that, though, perhaps there is a theological hurdle for some to get over: the very fact that God is the one who does the choosing. Yes, this brings us into the discussion (distasteful to some) of predestination, or more accurately—since we are speaking in terms of salvation— election. R. C. Sproul accurately describes the feeling of most people toward the concept: "The very word *pre-destination* has an ominous ring to it. It is linked to the despairing notion of fatalism and somehow suggests that

---

1. Martin Luther, *Commentary on the Epistle to the Galatians*, trans. Theodore Graebner (Grand Rapids: Zondervan, 1949), 20.

within its pale we are reduced to meaningless puppets. The word conjures up visions of a diabolical deity who plays capricious games with our lives."[2]

Sadly, this is what many people think about God's sovereign work and electing prerogative. It is a hard truth to come to terms with, but such a fatalistic view tragically eclipses the beauty of God's work for undeserving and incapable sinners in the gospel. Though space restricts a full-fledged treatment of the doctrine, it is important to note a few things, especially since predestination is inseparable from union with Christ. I want to say just three things for now.

A Biblical Doctrine

First, the doctrine is *biblical*. This should seem evident enough, as it is clearly spelled out in the section of Ephesians 1 quoted at the beginning of the chapter. Nor is this the only place we run up against the concept in Scripture. Just a few verses later on Paul will say—even more bluntly—that we have been "predestined according to the purpose of Him who works all things according to the counsel of His will" (Eph. 1:11). In Romans 8:29–30 we read, "For whom He foreknew, He also predestined to be conformed to the image of His Son, that He might be the firstborn among many brethren. Moreover whom He predestined, these He also called; whom He called, these He also justified; and whom He justified, these He also glorified." The Ephesians

2. R. C. Sproul, *Chosen by God* (Carol Stream, Ill.: Tyndale House, 1982), 1.

and Romans passages are places in which these theological terms are used explicitly, but if we broaden our radar to also pick up allusions to and themes of choosing, predetermining, and electing, the list gets longer.

There are some people who have a false notion of predestination—namely, that it was the invention of some ancient French "madman" named John Calvin. Probably Calvin would mourn that history has dubbed this doctrine "Calvinism," as though it somehow belonged more to him than to God.

Other people who are more informed would recognize that the idea of predestination is not strictly Calvinist and is a scriptural concept. Indeed, Catholics, Lutherans, Methodists, and so-called Calvinists all hold to different nuances of predestination. But even then, the most common view is not the biblical one: that is, while God does choose some to salvation, He does so based on "foreseen faith." This view states that God was able to look down the halls of time and see everyone who would, if presented the opportunity, respond to the gospel in faith. Those who would respond in faith God elects to everlasting life. This effectively makes our choice the foundation for God's. It would put us over and above God.

A Big Doctrine

To those who would argue for that view, I would respond that it does not square with the rest of the biblical data regarding who God is and that those who hold to it don't understand the second thing about predestination: it is a *big* doctrine. By that I mean several things. It is big in the sense that there is a lot at stake—like salvation. But the doctrine also deals with a big topic: the sovereignty of God. Or, to put it another way, election is a big deal because it deals with the *bigness* of God.

The Westminster Confession of Faith gives us a great description of what God's sovereignty is all about: "God, from all eternity, did, by the most wise and holy counsel of his own will, freely, and unchangeably ordain whatsoever comes to pass" (33.1). This sweeping statement accurately captures the bigness of God, all in reference to predestination. It captures His bigness first, in terms of time: "from all eternity"—there was never a moment that God wasn't in control; second, in terms of necessity: "freely"—no one forces God to do anything; third, in terms of permanence: "unchangeably"—nothing can thwart God's plan or cause it to take a detour; and fourth, in terms of scope: "whatsoever comes to pass"—in other words, if it happened, it is because God ordained it to happen.

If we lose God's bigness, we lose God. If God is not sovereign, He is not God at all. If something can be decided or determined apart from, outside of, or before God, then that means there is something greater than God. And if something is greater than God, then God isn't God. Think about it: Why would you want to choose salvation in Jesus for yourself when it would mean putting your eternal destiny in the hands of a God who has less power than you?

The main concern for some people is that if we acknowledge God's sovereignty, then we are giving away our own freedom. But this is a false dilemma. Loraine Boettner writes, "The true solution of this difficult question respecting the sovereignty of God and the freedom of man, is not to be found in the denial of either, but rather in such reconciliation as gives full weight to each, yet which assigns a preeminence to the divine sovereignty corresponding to the infinite exaltation of the Creator above the sinful creature."[3] The same God who has ordained "whatsoever comes to pass" has also ordained our freedom. We can both be free, me and God. He is just freer. As a father and a child are both free, yet the father's freedom outweighs the child's, so too does God give His creatures freedom within His own freedom.

A Beautiful Doctrine

This brings us to the third thing regarding predestination. Not only is it a biblical doctrine and a big doctrine but it is also a *beautiful* doctrine. It can so often be caricatured as nothing more than a cold and lifeless calculus. But what does Paul say in Ephesians 1? That it was "in love" He predestined us (vv. 4–5). Thus it has been said that election is based on affection. God's love for us causes Him to ordain us to everlasting life. This is a beautiful truth and should move us to praise, as it does Paul: "Blessed be the God and Father of our Lord Jesus Christ!" (v. 3).

When properly understood, election teaches us not just about how great God is but about how good He is. He is a sovereign God, and yet a saving God. Some people might tend to pit John's "God is love" (1 John 4:16) against Paul's

---

3. Loraine Boettner, *The Reformed Doctrine of Predestination* (Phillipsburg, N.J.: P&R, 1932), 208.

predestination. But they go hand in hand. If God were not love, we would be lost. Yet while we were still sinners, God loved us—God *chose* us. "God's love is the fountainhead of the gospel. God's Son did not come into the world to persuade the Father to love or to win His love for us; He came as the gift of the Father's love to us."[4]

He Chose Us

This then brings us back to our initial question: Why would God choose me? How can it be that if faced with the option I would not choose God—who is only all good all the time—and yet He would choose me, even though I am only all sin? If the pervading principle of making a good choice is choosing good things, then why would God choose me? Quite simply, it is for His glory. Paul says as much in this passage: "He chose us…to the praise of the glory of His grace" (Eph. 1:4, 6).

This is not the first time Scripture presents to us a God who seems to make strange decisions. In many ways the opening of Ephesians reflects a well-known text in Deuteronomy regarding God's choice of the nation of Israel:

> For you are a holy people to the LORD your God; the LORD your God has chosen you to be a people for Himself, a special treasure above all the peoples on the face of the earth. The LORD did not set His love on you nor choose you because you were more in number than any other people, for you were the least of all

4 Ian Hamilton, *Ephesians* (Grand Rapids: Reformation Heritage Books, 2018), 20.

peoples; but because the LORD loves you, and because
He would keep the oath which He swore to your
fathers, the LORD has brought you out with a mighty
hand, and redeemed you from the house of bondage,
from the hand of Pharaoh king of Egypt. (7:6–8)

Note the similarities between these two passages.
While implicit in Ephesians, Deuteronomy draws out
clearly why God's electing choice seems odd: because Israel
was "the least of all peoples." There was nothing particularly impressive about this band of Hebrews, just as there is
nothing impressive about a band of wretched sinners. Yet
God saves, both passages tell us, out of love, for the sake of
sanctification, and ultimately to glorify Himself.

God's will is to own a people for Himself who would
be "holy and without blame" (Eph. 1:4)—a people who are
markedly different from the rest of the world, defined by
virtue and not vice. What better way to display His own
power and might and glory than to transform helpless sinners into saints? If we think there is something worthwhile
in us that caused God to choose us, then we have missed
the point. God chose us for the praise of His grace. If there
was something in us that earned salvation, it would not be
grace at all.

But once we realize that there is nothing in us that
makes us a fitting choice, not only do we see God's grace
but we see God's *glorious* grace—or, "the glory of His
grace" (Eph. 1:6). It all must go back to Him. God's choice
magnifies His glory and decimates our pride: "But God has
chosen the foolish things of the world to put to shame the
wise, and God has chosen the weak things of the world to

put to shame the things which are mighty; and the base things of the world and the things which are despised God has chosen, and the things which are not, to bring to nothing the things that are, that no flesh should glory in His presence" (1 Cor. 1:27–29). No one should glory, or boast, before the Lord, to whom all glory rightly belongs.

He Chose Us in Him

So we have seen thus far that God does the choosing and that for His own glory's sake He has chosen us. But then note last that all of this work has been done *in Christ*. These few words from Paul in Ephesians 1 open the door to the grandest concepts of salvation that Scripture reveals to us. When Paul tells us that this choosing took place "before the foundation of the world" (Eph. 1:4), he sends us into the marvelous and mysterious eternal counsel of the Godhead. More specifically, Paul refers to what theologians call the covenant of redemption. A *covenant* is a binding agreement between two or more parties. The covenant of redemption teaches us that the Trinity made a binding agreement before time began that the Father would send the Son who, equipped by the Spirit, would redeem the elect.

While it might sound overly heady and perhaps even speculative, the covenant of redemption can be understood simply by stating it this way: Christ came to the world with a purpose. He had an agenda. He had in mind a particular people to save. The redemption of sinners was not wishful thinking on His part, nor were the saved selected by lottery.

Jesus speaks of this intention in John 17, in what is known as the High Priestly Prayer:

> Jesus spoke these words, lifted up His eyes to heaven, and said: "Father, the hour has come. Glorify Your Son, that Your Son also may glorify You, as You have given Him authority over all flesh, that He should give eternal life to as many as You have given Him. And this is eternal life, that they may know You, the only true God, and Jesus Christ whom You have sent. I have glorified You on the earth. I have finished the work which You have given Me to do. And now, O Father, glorify Me together with Yourself, with the glory which I had with You before the world was." (vv. 1–5)

Jesus came to give eternal life to all whom the Father had given Him. This is the mission Jesus was on, or, as He says, "the work which You have given Me to do" (John 17:4; cf. John 6:37–39). Paul's words in the opening of Ephesians fill in the picture of what Jesus is referring to here—namely, that to be chosen in Christ means to be part of the eternal will of the Trinity for the redemption of humankind.

Ponder that for a moment. It is a breathtaking thought. Before you knew the gospel. Before you knew grammar. Before you could walk. Before you were born. Before you were conceived. Before your parents' generation, and their parents' generation. Before every significant moment in history. Before time itself—*you* were part of God's will. The triune God covenanted a plan of redemption: that the Father would save you by sending His Son in the power of the Spirit.

Even through all eternity God was contemplating us—but He was always contemplating us in Christ. If it weren't for this last bit, it would be a terrifying thought. But thanks be to God for our Lord Jesus Christ! The Father's love was toward us because His love has always been toward His Son. Wilhelmus à Brakel notes, "Love moved the Father and love moved the Lord Jesus. It is a covenant of love between those whose love proceeds within themselves, without there being any lovableness in the object of this love."[5] God was thinking of us not in and of ourselves, and certainly not in and of our sin, but truly in and of His Son. We are in His Son in the sense that we were the people given to His Son. He came to earth to represent us. He came to earth for us. Jesus came to save His body, His bride, the church (Eph. 5:23, 25)—the people whom He has been united to and appointed to represent since eternity.

There is a right and proper sense in which we must say we are not united to Christ until we put our faith in Him. That is, without faith we have no Spirit to draw us to and into Christ. The Westminster Shorter Catechism says the Spirit applies the saving benefits of redemption to us "by working faith in us and thereby uniting us to Christ" (30). But there is another sense in which it is right to say we have always been united to Christ. Spiritually, really and truly, we have no union until we have faith. But by means of representing us and our sorry state, our poor condition, we have been united to Christ ever since God chose us in Him

---

5. As quoted in J. V. Fesko, *The Trinity and the Covenant of Redemption* (Fearn, Ross-shire, Scotland: Mentor, 2016), 43.

before the foundations of the world. Even before coming to earth in the incarnation, the second person of the Trinity was already standing in our place, representing us in the eternal counsels of the Godhead.

Conclusion

We will never properly understand the doctrine of election if we don't take to heart those two precious words *in Him*. Apart from union with Christ, election would make no sense and could truly never have taken place. If God would not love us in His Son, He could not love us at all. So that is why when we consider this topic we must always do so with an eye to Christ. John Calvin wisely states that "we shall not find assurance of our election in ourselves; and not even in God the Father, if we conceive him as severed from his Son. Christ, then, is the mirror wherein we must, and without self-deception may, contemplate our own election."[6]

Election doesn't need to be an intimidating or offensive topic. God's choice is not arbitrary, cold, cruel, or foolish. God still abides by that basic principle of choosing: He chose what was best—because He chose His Son. True, there is no lovableness in us. But when God set His affection on us, He did so by selecting us in His Son—His *beloved* Son, with whom He is well pleased (Matt. 3:17). And that makes us beloved sons as well, for what He saw in us was everything that Christ one day would do for us.

This is what it means to be chosen in Christ. This is what it means to have an identity that is found in Christ,

---

6. Calvin, *Institutes*, 3.24.5.

and not in ourselves. How often we try to find our worth in our own accomplishments, the trophies on the shelf, the likes we get on Facebook, our looks—and how often we end up disappointed! Why? Because the "identity gospel" is a lie. None of those things can give us a true and lasting sense of value and worth. We can never accomplish enough, win enough, be popular enough, be attractive enough. These things can never confer upon us a sense that we are intrinsically and eternally valuable.

The gospel sweeps away all those poor attempts to find worth in ourselves and our own works when it announces the news that the God of the universe freely sought us out, set His heart on us in love, and chose us.

Questions for Further Study

1. What are some important choices you have made in life? What factors went into your decisions?

2. How is the doctrine of predestination biblical, big, and beautiful?

3. What does predestination teach us about God's love and grace?

4. How does the covenant of redemption teach us we are chosen in Christ?

5. How does the knowledge that we are chosen by God strip away false identities that are built on our own accomplishments and success?

PARDONED *in* HIM

*There is therefore now no condemnation to those who
are in Christ Jesus.*

—ROMANS 8:1

In January 2018 I watched the live coverage as the sentencing in Larry Nassar's very public trial was finally handed down. Nassar was the well-known USA Gymnastics national team doctor who, after nearly three decades, was finally caught in an unimaginable sexual abuse scandal that affected more than 160 young women. Defeated, gaunt, and exhausted, Nassar stood to hear the ruling from the judge: 40 to 175 years in prison. I will always remember the words of Judge Rosemarie Aquilina: "I have just signed your death warrant." Next, she had to quiet the courtroom as her words were met with praise and approval from those watching in person, many of whom were victims.

The sighs of relief, the cheers, and the applause—not just in that room but all over the country—said something powerful about the human race: we have a *need* for justice. In a time when our nation is divided on nearly every topic and sociopolitical issue conceivable, here was something strangely unifying. We loved witnessing the vindication of the innocent victims and the merciless punishment of the undeniably guilty. This is natural to us. You don't need to teach children to feel hurt or indignant when something wrong happens to them. We innately have a need to see wrongs righted, the guilty condemned, and the innocent set free.

But we also have the tendency to be inconsistent with this need and desire for justice. For if it were us standing in the place of the defendant—defeated, gaunt, exhausted, and knowing full well our guilt—then we would not want justice; we would want mercy. This is the case for us spiritually speaking, isn't it? As miserable offenders against God's law, we fully expect to hear God speak to us those same chilling words of Judge Aquilina: "I have just signed your death warrant." And He would be right to do so. That would be just, and in any other scenario justice is what we want. But we don't want it in this scenario, where the weight of justice would crush us. In this scenario, we want mercy.

In Romans 8:1, in a single, concise sentence Paul reveals to us how God is able to give both justice and mercy. He is able to execute justice and maintain His own righteousness, but He is also able to grant us the mercy we so desperately need. It seems like a contradiction. After all, how could God possibly be just and simultaneously let the guilty go free? The answer is found, of course, *in Christ*. That is what Romans 8:1 unpacks for us: "There is therefore now no condemnation to those who are in Christ Jesus." It would be hard to overstate how crucial grasping this concept is for understanding the Christian life. Truly, this one verse gives us "the theme of the entire Word of God. Indeed, it is the gospel's very heart."[1]

Natural Justice

The Bible is not shy regarding the attribute of God's justice, or righteousness:

> He is the Rock, His work is perfect;
> For all His ways are justice,
> A God of truth and without injustice;
> Righteous and upright is He. (Deut. 32:4)

"For the LORD is righteous, He loves righteousness" (Ps. 11:7). God Himself says, "I, the LORD, love justice" (Isa. 61:8). And it is because God loves justice and righteousness that we too have an instinctive desire for justice and righteousness. We were made in His image. We reflect the character of our Creator, especially in terms of "knowledge, righteousness, and true holiness" (Westminster Confession of Faith 4.2; cf. Eph. 4:24; Col. 3:10).

Calling a Line Crooked

If God did not inscribe right and wrong on our hearts, we would have no sense of these things. C. S. Lewis famously made this observation, recalling the inconsistencies of his atheism: "My argument against God was that the universe seems so cruel and unjust. But how did I get this idea of

---

1. James Montgomery Boice, *The Reign of Grace (Romans 5–8)*, Boice Expositional Commentary 22 (Grand Rapids: Baker, 1992), 789.

just, unjust? A man does not call a line crooked unless he first has some idea of straight. What was I comparing the universe to when I called it unjust?"[2] Lewis has touched on what Scripture teaches: that in creating us, God has revealed to us His moral law. He has given us the straight line so we can know the crooked.

Good theology will tell you that you don't need the Bible to know how to live a "good" or "upright" life. The knowledge of what is "good" and "upright" comes to us naturally (although the ability to put that knowledge into action does not). Paul says as much earlier in Romans: "For when Gentiles, who do not have the law, by nature do the things in the law, these, although not having the law, are a law to themselves, who show the work of the law written in their hearts, their conscience also bearing witness, and between themselves their thoughts accusing or else excusing them" (2:14–15). Gentiles, or pagans, who do not have the moral law (the Ten Commandments) and yet live by them prove that before God's law was ever written on stone tablets, it was written on their hearts (see Eccl. 7:29).

Knowing and Doing What Is Right— Are We Capable of Either?

The problem, as I've said, is that although we know what is right, we so rarely do what is right. If we are being honest, we know that "all have sinned" and that "there is none righteous" (Rom. 3:23, 10, respectively) and that we stand guilty

2. C. S. Lewis, *Mere Christianity* (New York: HarperCollins, 2001), 38.

before the Judge: Almighty God in heaven. As we look at ourselves and the lives we lead, we know there is nothing we can bring to the table that would warrant any kind of commendation—only condemnation.

As I said, this takes honest self-reflection and assessment. In our day, many people thoughtlessly presume they have no need to change and that they are inherently good—to imply otherwise is insulting. This is part of the cultural identity crisis we are going through: many people assume that they are good, and therefore that entitles them to make any lifestyle decision they want, free from the judgment of others. If it seems right to them, that's because it must be right. No one dare say otherwise.

But let me say otherwise: we think evil thoughts, we say hurtful things, and we simply do bad stuff. This is what Thomas Cranmer summed up so beautifully in his famous prayer of confession: "Almighty and most merciful Father, we have erred and strayed from thy ways like lost sheep, we have followed too much the devices and desires of our own hearts. We have offended against thy holy laws: We have left undone those things which we ought to have done, and we have done those things which we ought not to have done, *and there is no health in us.*"[3]

This is the reality of humanity that Scripture reveals to us: there is no spiritual good in us. We are so entrenched in our sins and trespasses that Scripture is right to say we are dead in them (Eph. 2:1). The judgment, therefore, is a

---

3. From the morning prayer liturgy in Cranmer's 1559 Book of Common Prayer. *The Book of Common Prayer: The Texts of 1549, 1559, and 1662* (London: Oxford, 2011), 103 (emphasis added).

fitting conclusion to that reality: "The wages of sin is death" (Rom. 6:23). We stand condemned before the Judge with a death sentence hanging over us. Hence, Lewis appropriately says that "[the Christian religion] does not begin in comfort but in dismay."[4]

But the comfort does come, and it comes beautifully in Romans 8:1: "There is therefore now no condemnation to those who are in Christ Jesus." When Paul says that there is "no condemnation" for us, it is another way of saying there is no death sentence. We have received a pardon. But how can that be? Isn't the guilty getting off free the kind of thing that gets our ire up precisely because God built us with a passion for justice? How can the same God who says, "I love justice" let guilty sinners go? Doesn't that spit in the face of justice? Is God not violating His own ethic and standard? Isn't He ignoring the intrinsic qualities of straight and crooked with which He endowed us? Isn't that, by definition, *un*just?

And the answer is, shockingly, no.

Supernatural Mercy

The verse does not read "There is therefore now no condemnation." Period. Full stop. As if God throws out any and all concepts of justice, punishment, or comeuppance for the wicked. What it says is that there is no condemnation "*to those who are in Christ Jesus.*" That is, if people are not in Christ Jesus, they can expect the full weight of God's judgment to fall on them on the last day (Matt. 25:46).

---

4. Lewis, *Mere Christianity*, 32.

Is There Injustice on God's Part?

But why do those people who are "in Christ" get a pass? Are not Christians just as sinful as non-Christians and therefore equally deserving of God's wrath and punishment? Yes. As Puritan Matthew Poole states, Paul is not asserting that "there is no matter of condemnation, or nothing damnable in them that are in Christ, there is enough and enough of that."[5] So yes, we deserve condemnation, but the glorious good news of the gospel is that to be in Christ means that Christ takes the blow for us. We are "hidden with Christ" (Col. 3:3), and therefore the divine punishment—"the wages of sin"—cannot reach us. There is no condemnation for those who are in Christ Jesus precisely because Jesus was condemned in our place.

This might sound like the absolute paragon of injustice: a judge placing the penalty for someone's wrongdoing on another person, making him an unwitting scapegoat. Maybe so, except that in this instance *Jesus volunteered* to be our scapegoat.

In the last chapter I talked about the covenant of redemption, that eternal plan of the Trinity to save the elect. Part of that plan involved the Son coming to this earth to take the divine penalty for His people's sins. In the eternal counsel of God, the words of the Father and Judge could be heard to the Son: "I have just signed your death warrant." This was the cost of our redemption. This is what it would take to reconcile us to God: that Christ would pay

---

5. Matthew Poole, *Commentary on the Bible* (1685; repr., Edinburgh: Banner of Truth, 1979), 3:502.

the wages of our sin. "For Christ also suffered once for sins, the just for the unjust, that He might bring us to God, being put to death in the flesh" (1 Peter 3:18). This is why Christ came: that He might receive the brunt of God's relentless justice in order that we might receive the blessing of God's relentless grace.

Though the concept was somewhat veiled at first, from its beginning the Bible reveals that the Son would be sent to suffer. Genesis 3:15 prophesies the coming Messiah as one who would defeat the wicked serpent but be bruised, or wounded, in the process. Isaiah 53:4–6 gives us even more detail about the nature of Christ's suffering as substitutionary:

> Surely He has borne our griefs
> And carried our sorrows;
> Yet we esteemed Him stricken,
> Smitten by God, and afflicted.
> But He was wounded for our transgressions,
> He was bruised for our iniquities;
> The chastisement for our peace was upon Him,
> And by His stripes we are healed.
> All we like sheep have gone astray;
> We have turned, every one, to his own way;
> And the LORD has laid on Him the iniquity of us all.

This passage shouts at us about our union with Christ. It tells us in vivid language what Christ gets from being united to us. Notice the pronouns: He gets *our* grief, *our* sorrows, piercings for *our* transgressions, chastisement that brings *us* peace, the iniquity of *us all*. And what do we receive from being united with Him? Peace and healing. We receive no condemnation.

Christ came to be our substitute, to stand in our place and take the wrath of God for our sin. Paul even alludes to this in the verses following Romans 8:1 when He says that we are free from condemnation because "[God sent] His own Son in the likeness of sinful flesh, on account of sin" (v. 3). The Old Testament prophesied this, the New Testament authors confirmed it, and Jesus Himself taught it explicitly to His disciples: "The Son of Man must suffer many things, and be rejected by the elders and chief priests and scribes, and be killed" (Luke 9:22).

The Passive Obedience of Christ

Notice that Jesus does not say His mission was simply to come and be killed but first to "suffer many things." The price for our sin was paid not only at the cross but also throughout Jesus's entire life. As He left the riches, the glories, and—yes—even the comforts of heaven, He did so to come and live a life marked by misery on this sin-bound earth. Even from His birth, Christ came to bear our grief and carry our sorrows (Matt. 8:17)—to know our weaknesses and be tempted in every respect as we are, yet without sin (Heb. 4:15).[6] Theologians call this the *passive obedience* of Christ—not passive in the sense that He didn't

---

6. Westminster Shorter Catechism 27 asks, "Wherein did Christ's humiliation consist?" Answer: "Christ's humiliation consisted in his being born, and that in a low condition, made under the law, undergoing the miseries of this life, the wrath of God, and the cursed death of the cross; in being buried, and continuing under the power of death for a time."

do anything, but passive in its original meaning, which comes from the Latin *passio*, "to suffer."

I said previously that when God chose us in Christ that meant He saw in us everything that Christ would one day do for us. Part of what Christ did for us was suffer. Though this was not restricted to the cross, it certainly culminated there. At the cross the Father threw the entire weight of His wrath against His beloved, perfectly obedient Son. As Jesus hung from the cross—defeated, gaunt, and exhausted, knowing full well His innocence—He cried to His heavenly Father, and yet there came no reply. That deafening silence was a certain guarantee that Jesus had been condemned in our place. In this way God maintained His justice and righteousness—no sins went unpunished. Christ fulfilled the justice of God by enduring the agony of death. And this was all done in love: "But God demonstrates His own love toward us, in that while we were still sinners, Christ died for us" (Rom. 5:8). While we were still sinners, while we were still condemnable wretches, the Father sent His Son to step in and take our punishment.

Safe in Christ

In some feeble attempt to grasp the height and depth of this love—which truly does surpass all knowledge (Eph. 3:18–19)—we need to see ourselves on the cross. We need to imagine the entire weight of God's wrath thrown at us. We need to recognize the horrors of hell that Christ underwent for our sake at Golgotha. For the sobering reality is this: if I am not in Christ, I am dead. The protection from

God's condemnation extends only to those who look to Jesus by faith and are therefore hid in Him. If Jesus doesn't take the blow, then we do. The cross is what could have been—*should have been*—my experience, my reality, my torture. But by faith, the only crucifixion I will ever know is the one Christ endured for me—"I have been crucified with Christ" (Gal. 2:20).

This is the essence behind one of the most famous lines on union with Christ in theology, coming from John Calvin: "First, we must understand that as long as Christ remains outside of us, and we are separated from him, all that he has suffered and done for the salvation of the human race remains useless and of no value to us."[7] If we are not united to Christ, His suffering is worthless to us. His death will not spare us ours. It doesn't matter how "good" we are, how often we go to church, how often we pray, what charities we give to—none of it matters if Christ is not dwelling in us, and we in Him. As long as He remains outside of us we will still be condemned because God must punish every sin.

But to be in Christ—that is the greatest comfort imaginable! There is no place more secure than to be in Christ. In Christ we are saved from the curse of sin because Christ took the curse for us (Gal. 3:13). Do you see how crucial this union is? It is only when we are in Christ that we can meaningfully sing those climactic words of Charles Wesley's grand hymn "And Can It Be": "No condemnation now I dread; Jesus, and all in Him is mine!"[8]

---

7. Calvin, *Institutes*, 3.1.1.
8. Charles Wesley, "And Can It Be" (1738), in the public domain.

This is our reality *now*—we now possess the guarantee of a free pardon from God's holy and just judgment because we are found in the penalty-bearing Son. This is our identity. Our pardon is part of who we are; we are no longer confined to eke out a pathetic existence on death row, but can live in the robust freedom of full forgiveness in Jesus. This should give us joy, confidence, and boldness. "The godly have an invincible fortress, for [we] know that while [we] abide in Christ [we] are beyond every danger of condemnation."[9]

Conclusion

In the case of Larry Nassar, Rachael Denhollander received international recognition as the first victim to step forward and truly get the investigation under way. A mother of two, practicing attorney, and former gymnast, Denhollander pursued justice while others turned a blind eye. Her motivation was rooted predominantly in her Christian faith. She had that innate desire for wrongs to be righted, for the guilty to be caught and punished for their crimes— and she knew this desire came because she was made in the image of a just God.

But as a self-professed sinner, Denhollander also knew of the need for mercy. And in her victim impact statement, Denhollander invited Nassar to experience a different kind of justice than he would ever experience in a human court. She invited him to see the Judge who would not say to

9. John Calvin, *Commentaries on the Epistle to the Romans*, in *Calvin's Commentaries* (Grand Rapids: Baker, 1981), 19:276.

him, "I have just signed your death warrant," but instead who would say, "I have just signed my Son's death warrant for you." This is what Denhollander said in her statement, speaking directly to Nassar:

> Should you ever reach the point of truly facing what you have done, the guilt will be crushing. And that is what makes the gospel of Christ so sweet. Because it extends grace and hope and mercy where none should be found. And it will be there for you. I pray you experience the soul crushing weight of guilt so you may someday experience true repentance and true forgiveness from God, which you need far more than forgiveness from me—though I extend that to you as well.[10]

Denhollander could forgive because she knew she had been forgiven. She knew that in Christ there was no condemnation against her. And that reality is offered freely to everyone, regardless of the sin or the sinner, because of the love and mercy of God.

Are you in Christ, my friend? Know that it is only by being united to Him that you will escape the wrath of God that you deserve for your many sins. Cover yourself in Christ as He takes the blow of God's justice so you may receive the blessing of God's grace and mercy.

---

10. As quoted in Justin Taylor, "The Incredible Testimony as a Former Gymnast Confronts Her Sexual Abuser in Court," *Between Two Worlds* (blog), The Gospel Coalition, January 24, 2018, https://www.thegospelcoalition.org/blogs/justin-taylor/incredible-testimony-former-gymnast-confronts-sexual-abuser-court/.

Questions for Further Study

1. Why does every human desire justice? Why does every human desire mercy?

2. What does Scripture say about the attribute of God's justice?

3. What does Isaiah 53:4–6 teach us about union with Christ?

4. What is the *passive obedience* of Christ?

5. How does an identity founded on forgiveness in Christ excel other identities that the world tries to offer us?

RIGHTEOUS *in* HIM

*For He made Him who knew no sin to be sin for us,
that we might become the righteousness of God in Him.*
—2 CORINTHIANS 5:21

What gets you into heaven? In the last chapter we looked at the forgiveness that is ours in Christ Jesus. We saw that the only reason we can receive the mercy of God is because Christ took the unfiltered just punishment of God in our place. For Christ there was a curse and a cross; for us there is forgiveness. But is forgiveness all we need to be saved? Will divine forgiveness get us into heaven? The answer is no. Perhaps that sounds odd to you, but it is the truth. Let's look at why.

If someone is not in Christ, they are automatically "in Adam." That is, Adam as the first human being is representative of the entire human race. What is true of him is true for us. First Corinthians 15:22 tells us that is not exactly good news—rather, "in Adam all die." That was Adam's forewarned punishment if he were to eat of the forbidden fruit: "for in the day that you eat of it you shall surely die"

(Gen. 2:17). Adam did not obey and therefore was not able to obtain the righteousness necessary to taste of the tree of life (Gen. 3:22). Adam's curse and restriction became our reality, as we are "in him." This tells us that Adam's sin has brought a twofold necessity: first, we must be forgiven our iniquities; second, we must be granted a *positive righteousness*. Another way to put it, in keeping with our look at Genesis, is to say we need to be both forgiven for eating the forbidden fruit and granted access to eat the living fruit. Both forgiveness and righteousness are necessary to stand before God. Psalm 24:3–4 asks, "Who may ascend into the hill of the LORD? Or who may stand in His holy place?" The answer: "He who has clean hands and a pure heart." We not only need forgiveness for being caught red-handed in sin, but we also need those hands cleansed, purified, and made righteous.

This can't happen "in Adam," but it can happen "in Christ." Christ came as the second (or last) Adam and succeeded where the first failed, and that is why we need to be found in Him. We need to be in this second Adam who has walked in our skin, yet was sinless and prevailed against the world, the flesh, and the devil. The only way we can get into heaven is to have His positive righteousness.

A Righteousness Earned by Christ

So Christ comes in our flesh and blood, as the second Adam, to rescue us from the grip of sin. If we think of it in accounting terms, we could say that sin puts us in the red, in debt. We saw in the last chapter that our union with Christ entailed His condemnation for our pardon. This pardon balances the books. But to be in the black, to have a positive credit, we need righteousness. No righteousness means no heaven—no matter how balanced the books may be. Yet our God is so good that He gives us His Son, who not only takes on our punishment but also gives us His reward. He gives us the righteousness that He earned. Second Corinthians 5:21 is the perfect text to teach us this marvelous truth: "For He made Him who knew no sin to be sin for us, that we might become the righteousness of God in Him."

The Glorious Exchange

Theologians have often referred to the doctrine contained in this verse as the "glorious exchange." For centuries in the early church the idea of this exchange was the predominant way people spoke of and understood the concept of justification. This perhaps goes back as far as the late first- or early second-century anonymous letter known as the *Epistle to Diognetus*, where we read, "O sweet exchange, O the incomprehensible work of God, O the unexpected blessings, that the sinfulness of many should be hidden in one righteous person, while the righteousness of one should justify many sinners!"[1]

Other early church fathers like Ignatius, Polycarp, and Irenaeus used this motif frequently as well. What these ancient theologians understood is that this exchange

---

1. As quoted in Michael Horton, *Justification* (Grand Rapids: Zondervan, 2019), 1:45. For a full treatment of the exchange motif in the early church, see 39–74.

imagery captured the heart of justification: what is Christ's becomes ours; what is ours becomes His. He receives all our filth and sin and guilt; we receive every spiritual blessing in the heavenly places. We receive His perfect righteousness. This, in a nutshell, is what it means to be justified.

Does it mean we literally become righteous, as if something within us changes and we are the righteousness of God? No, just as nothing literally changed within Jesus to make Him sin on the cross. As Phillip P. Bliss has so memorably phrased it, "In my place condemned He stood."[2] It was in our place: Christ was condemned not for His sin, not for literally becoming sin, but for *representing* our sin. That's the key. In the eyes of God, the Son was sin on the cross—that is how truly, intimately, unashamedly Jesus took our sin for us. That is how firmly He stood in our place. Likewise, we do not become intrinsically righteous—that cannot happen this side of heaven. But when we have sincere faith, in the eyes of God we are viewed as righteous as Jesus.

Did you catch that? Maybe your eyes scanned right over the words without really allowing your heart to take it in. Here it is again: in the sight of God, the Christian is reckoned to be as righteous as Christ! What a marvel! Does it not buckle your knees, fill your soul, and cause you to cry out in praise to our gracious God?

Living He Loved and Justified Me
Our justification requires the death of Christ just as much as it requires His life. There is a woeful misconception of

---

2. Philip P. Bliss, "Man of Sorrows" (1875), in the public domain.

this in mainstream Christianity today. It is easy to focus predominantly—if not exclusively—on the cross of Christ and to preach of His sacrificial death for us unworthy sinners. But the death of Jesus is nothing without the life of Jesus. Perhaps that seems like such a simplistic statement that it is not worth saying, but it needs to be stressed. The death of Jesus means nothing to us if it does not come with His perfect life and His vindicating resurrection. The hope of the gospel would really be a mirage because it could not offer us anything beyond this life. The death of Christ keeps us out of hell, but it doesn't get us into heaven.

It makes no logical sense to overlook, underplay, or even exclude the importance of the perfect life of Christ. It was His sinless living that made His selfless death saving! If Jesus had not lived a perfect life, then His death on the cross—no matter how loving and sacrificial—would not have been able to merit us anything eternal. It is through His life that He earned heaven for us. Therefore, we need to garner an appropriate appreciation for the life of Jesus. As we read the Gospel accounts, we need to see someone who came to *live for us*. We need to see someone whose every breath, every thought, every movement, every action, was truly done *for us*. And it was all perfection. Just as our every breath, thought, movement, and action are tainted with sin, Christ's were all sinless. That was what He came to do, after all: to be sinless, perfectly obedient, righteous for us.

In the last chapter we considered Christ's *passive obedience*: every way in which He was humbled by suffering for our sake. It refers to Him taking on the curse of sin for us. But now we are referring to Christ's *active obedience*: every way in which Christ was perfectly obedient in our place. Christ's active obedience is His impeccable dedication to the Father in everything that He ever did. It is Him coming as the second Adam: the One who will fully submit and obey in order to eat from the tree of life.

Fulfilling All Righteousness

A beautiful little verse in Matthew's Gospel has all this soul-saving truth packed into it. It is during the account of Jesus's baptism by John the Baptist in chapter 3:

> Then Jesus came from Galilee to John at the Jordan to be baptized by him. And John tried to prevent Him, saying, "I need to be baptized by You, and are You coming to me?"
>
> But Jesus answered and said to him, "Permit it to be so now, for thus it is fitting for us to fulfill all righteousness." (vv. 13–15)

It is this reply of Jesus that is so crucial for us to grasp: He found it fitting, proper, necessary, that He come to "fulfill all righteousness." R. C. Sproul explains well the importance of this passage:

> In all the New Testament, I do not think there is any more important text defining the work of Jesus. It tells us that Jesus was sent to fulfill all righteousness. For the Jews, that meant obeying every jot and tittle of the law. In undergoing baptism, Jesus was not acting for Himself but for His people. Since His people were required to keep the Ten Commandments, He had to keep the Ten Commandments. Likewise, since His people were now required, according to the com-

mand of the prophet John the Baptist, to submit to this baptismal ritual, He had to submit to it.

Then Sproul gets into what I have just been saying:

> Jesus had to adhere to the whole law of God because the redemption He brought was not accomplished solely by His death on the cross. God did not send Jesus to earth on Good Friday so He could go straight to the cross. *Jesus not only had to die for our sins, but also had to live for our righteousness.*[3]

A Righteousness Predicted by the Old Testament

When Jesus says that He comes to fulfill all righteousness, He is saying that this was something that had to be done. This should have come as no surprise to the Jews of Jesus's day. If they knew their Bibles (our Old Testaments) well, they would have been expecting a future servant who was marked primarily by one thing: righteousness. One of the most explicit passages that comes to mind is from the prophet Jeremiah:

> "Behold, the days are coming," says the LORD,
> "That I will raise to David a Branch of righteousness;
> A King shall reign and prosper,
> And execute judgment and righteousness in the earth.
> In His days Judah will be saved,
> And Israel will dwell safely;
> Now this is His name by which He will be called:
> THE LORD OUR RIGHTEOUSNESS. (Jer. 23:5–6)

---

3. R. C. Sproul, *The Work of Christ* (Colorado Springs: David C. Cook, 2012), 70–71 (emphasis added).

This is what the people of God were looking for in the promised Messiah: a righteous descendant of David who would rule righteously and be called "The Lord our righteousness." Other passages point to this as well:

> He shall see the labor of His soul, and be satisfied.
> By His knowledge My righteous Servant shall justify
> many,
> For He shall bear their iniquities. (Isa. 53:11)

> Seventy weeks are determined
> For your people and for your holy city,
> To finish the transgression,
> To make an end of sins,
> To make reconciliation for iniquity,
> *To bring in everlasting righteousness,*
> To seal up vision and prophecy,
> And to anoint the Most Holy. (Dan. 9:24)

> But to you who fear My name
> The Sun of Righteousness shall arise
> With healing in His wings;
> And you shall go out
> And grow fat like stall-fed calves. (Mal. 4:2)

One astounding text in this regard is Zechariah 3. Zechariah receives in a vision a graphic and gripping display of both the terror of being left in our sin and the joy of being found in the righteousness from God. In the vision, Zechariah sees Joshua the high priest, who represents the people of God, standing in the heavenly throne room dressed in filthy rags:

Then he showed me Joshua the high priest standing before the Angel of the LORD, and Satan standing at his right hand to oppose him. And the LORD said to Satan, "The LORD rebuke you, Satan! The LORD who has chosen Jerusalem rebuke you! Is this not a brand plucked from the fire?"

Now Joshua was clothed with filthy garments, and was standing before the Angel. (vv. 1–3)

It is a grim tale. Can you imagine being an Israelite and learning that the one person who is meant to represent you before almighty God was dressed in soiled clothes? Joshua does not have the clean hands of Psalm 24:4 that are required to stand before the Lord and live. He will be condemned, and all of Israel with him. This is why Satan is accusing him—and Satan is not wrong, which is the scary thing. But suddenly, God Himself intervenes:

Then He answered and spoke to those who stood before Him, saying, "Take away the filthy garments from him." And to him He said, "See, I have removed your iniquity from you, and I will clothe you with rich robes."

And I said, "Let them put a clean turban on his head."

So they put a clean turban on his head, and they put the clothes on him. And the Angel of the LORD stood by. (vv. 4–5)

Here we see that the filthy rags represent the filth of sin. But the Angel of the Lord removes the rags and gives Joshua new robes. In *Death in Adam, Life in Christ*, J. V. Fesko explains that "if the defiled garments represent sin, then the pure vestments represent, not merely the absence of sin, but the positive presence of righteousness."[4] You can be sure that the people of God got the message: in order to live, they needed clean clothes. They needed righteousness, and it was righteousness that they did not have in and of themselves. They needed righteousness from God.

And at His baptism, that is precisely what Jesus said He came to bring (Matt. 3:15). Interestingly, it is right after this, in verse 17, that the Father speaks from heaven for all to hear: "This is My beloved Son, in whom I am well pleased." He is stating at the start of Jesus's public ministry that Jesus has indeed done what He came to do: He has become righteousness for us (1 Cor. 1:30). The Father is essentially saying, "He is the one who will please me. You don't need to try. I am satisfied in Him!" If God is satisfied in Him, should we not be as well? If God will accept His righteousness, then should we not receive it by faith?

A Righteousness Received through Faith Alone

Incidentally, that is the only way we receive Christ's righteousness: by faith. When we receive the righteousness of Christ we are *justified*. Justification is the opposite of condemnation. Our sin condemns us, but the righteousness of Christ justifies us. That is, it puts us on right terms with God. Justification is what can allow us to ascend that holy hill of the Lord (Ps. 24:3). The Westminster Shorter Catechism defines justification by saying it is "an act of God's

---

4. J. V. Fesko, *Death in Adam, Life in Christ: The Doctrine of Imputation* (Fearn, Ross-shire, Scotland: Mentor, 2017), 190.

free grace, wherein he pardons all our sins, and accepts us as righteous in his sight, *only for the righteousness of Christ imputed to us, and received by faith alone*" (33, emphasis added). *Imputed* means "transferred" or "accounted to." What was transferred to us? The righteousness of Jesus Christ, which He merited in His faithful life on earth.

This is what you need to get when you consider the life of Christ: it was a life lived for you that you might live before God. God demands perfect obedience to His law. Simply being made in His image to reflect who He is requires such fidelity from us. And apart from this kind of obedience, the only thing we can expect is damnation. God expects us to "fulfill all righteousness," but sin renders that impossible.

Forsaking All, I Take Him

So what do we do? Do we just give up now? Do we resign ourselves to despair and await the inevitable death penalty? No! The gospel gives us great hope, and that hope lies entirely outside of ourselves in the person of Jesus Christ. For He came and "fulfilled all righteousness" for us. It is His perfection that saves, not ours. It is His obedience that saves, not ours. It is His righteousness that saves, not ours.

At the heart of the doctrine of union with Christ is actually a separation. It is a separation—a divorce—from ourselves in order that we might be united to Christ. We cannot serve two masters. We cannot belong to ourselves if we are to belong to Jesus. But by forsaking ourselves and seeing everything in Christ—which is what faith is—we truly receive everything that is in Christ. We receive His righteousness when we are united to Him. We are dressed in the spotless robe of His perfection because we are dressed in Him. In a 1535 lecture on Galatians, Luther was moved to praise by this union with Christ that we receive by faith alone. He said:

> But so far as justification is concerned, Christ and I must be so closely attached that He lives in me and I in Him. What a marvelous way of speaking! Because He lives in me, whatever grace, righteousness, life, peace, and salvation there is in me is all Christ's; nevertheless, it is mine as well, by the cementing and attachment that are through faith. In this way, Paul seeks to withdraw us from ourselves…and to transplant us into Christ and faith in Christ, so that in the area of justification we look only at grace, and separate it far from the Law and from works, which belong far away.[5]

Do you understand what Luther is saying? Do you believe what Luther is saying? Everything depends on whether or not you believe this fact: to be justified, to be righteous, we need to look entirely outside and away from ourselves and anything that we could ever hope to do. True faith is abhorring and rejecting anything in us and accepting everything that is in Christ. I love the helpful mnemonic FAITH: Forsaking All, I Take Him.

It has to be Jesus whom we look to. We are only righteous when we are in Him. Michael Horton captures the importance of this well. Bask in this glorious truth: "While

---

5. As quoted in *The Legacy of Luther*, ed. R. C. Sproul and Stephen J. Nichols (Orlando, Fla.: Reformation Trust, 2016), 136.

our righteousness is indeed external to us—an alien righteousness that belongs properly to Christ rather than to us—Christ himself does not remain alien, but joins himself to us and us to him."[6]

Do you see how important it is to be *in Christ*? Apart from Christ you are still in Adam. Adam remains your head, your captain—and his is not a team you want to be on. There is death in Adam, but life in Christ. Apart from Christ you can be defined only by your faults and failures. Why would you have that as your identity when you could make the exchange and be defined by the perfection of Jesus Christ?

Picture Perfect

Our society loves perfectionism. It thrives on it. And most of us are prone to it as well—otherwise why do we care so deeply that the pictures we post on social media are just so? Why do we get so anxious that our children be dressed like models from a clothing catalog and sit completely still in church without making a fuss? Why do we feel compelled to brag to our friends and neighbors about promotions or new cars or our children's achievements in school and sports, but we gloss over details about work troubles, old clunkers, or discipline troubles in the home?

We do this because we feel pressured to present a picture of perfection. We need people to think we have it all together. But we know the truth: we don't have anything

---

6. Michael S. Horton, *Covenant and Salvation: Union with Christ* (Louisville, Ky.: Westminster John Knox Press, 2007), 145.

together! It is almost all falling apart all the time. We want to be perfect so badly, but we can't do it. We can present only the illusion of perfection (and even that we so often do poorly). But we can't attain it on our own. We are too broken and sinful. There is no health in us. We have no perfection in ourselves, and our obsession with trying to fool people into thinking otherwise is slowly killing us.

Friend, don't hold on to what you have; it only leads to death. Take what Christ is freely offering you, which is Himself, so that "in Him [you] might become the righteousness of God." For that means life! In the words of Horatius Bonar, "Thy righteousness alone can clothe and beautify; I wrap it round my soul—in this I'll live and die."[7] There is life in Christ because He fulfilled all righteousness. There is life in Christ because of His perfect active obedience.

Conclusion

Maybe it is because of that truth—there is eternal life in the obedience of Christ—that J. Gresham Machen was thinking about the obedience of Jesus as he neared his earthly death. Machen was a remarkable man. A brilliant theologian, he secured a coveted teaching position at Princeton before he was thirty, founded a seminary before he was fifty, and helped form an entire denomination before he reached fifty-five. Yet just after Christmas in 1936, while he was on a preaching tour in the subzero temperatures of North Dakota, Machen contracted pneumonia. Machen

7. Horatius Bonar, "Thy Works, Not Mine, O Christ" (1862), in the public domain.

knew he was dying. He could barely breathe for the last two days of his life, but when he could manage the strength he would send off telegrams to friends and family back in Philadelphia who were tending to his seminary and other ministries. He even wrote a check to pay bills that were about to be past due. But in his final moment of clarity, he sent a telegram to his good friend and fellow professor John Murray and died hours later on New Year's Day 1937. The telegram read, "I am so thankful for the active obedience of Christ. No hope without it."

His biographer writes this: "Now that he realized that he was about to pass over the river into the eternal city…he gave expression to the conviction that he had assurance not only of remission of sin and its penalty but also of being accepted as perfectly obedient and righteous, and so an heir of eternal life, because of the perfect obedience of Christ."[8]

So what gets you into heaven?

---

8. Ned B. Stonehouse, *J. Gresham Machen* (1954; repr., Willow Grove, Pa.: The Committee for the Historian of the Orthodox Presbyterian Church, 2004), 451.

Questions for Further Study

1. What gets you into heaven?

2. Jesus came to "fulfill all righteousness" (Matt. 3:15). What does this mean?

3. What are some Old Testament passages that predicted the Messiah would come in righteousness?

4. How do we receive the righteousness of Christ?

5. How does the righteousness of Christ free us from pressures of perfectionism? In what other ways is an identity in Christ freeing?

5

ADOPTED *in* HIM

For you are all sons of God through faith in Christ Jesus.
—GALATIANS 3:26

"Our Father, who art in heaven…" These words echo in countless sanctuaries and worship halls around the world each Sunday as congregations recite this staple of historic Christian liturgy. We know it by heart, but do our hearts know it? I'm referring specifically to those opening two words: "Our Father." Do we truly understand what it means that we can call God our Father? As a pastor I have been saddened at how little this warm and assuring truth seems to have penetrated the lives of believers. And yet, as I hope to prove, there is no sweeter blessing than being part of God's family and having Him as our never-failing, never-leaving, everlasting Father.

When we refer to God as Father, we are talking about the first person of the Holy Trinity, and He is called Father because of His relation to the second person: He is "the God and Father of our Lord Jesus Christ" (1 Peter 1:3; cf. 2 Cor. 1:3; Eph. 1:3). And while it is true that Jesus is the only *begotten* Son of God, He is not the *only* son of God. On the contrary, as C. S. Lewis memorably put it, "the Son of God became a man to enable men to become sons of God."[1] Indeed, Paul goes on to say in Galatians 4:5 that the purpose for which God sent His Son was so that "we might receive the adoption as sons." The mission of redemption was to bring "many sons to glory" (Heb. 2:10), and this happens only through union with Christ.

This is what Paul says in Galatians 3:26 (quoted at the start of the chapter)—that through faith in Christ Jesus we are brought into such a vital and real communion with the Savior that we can receive the title that rightly belongs uniquely to Him: son of God. By the Spirit we are drawn into the divine family, allowing us to name Jesus as our brother and God as our father. This process is called, appropriately, adoption.

Adoption powerfully gets to the heart of what it means to be a Christian. According to John Murray, adoption is "surely the apex of grace and privilege."[2] If we don't grasp the concept of adoption, we have failed to grasp the relationship that we have with God. This inevitably will lead to frustrations and failings on our part. We will miss out on the bountiful blessings of belonging to God in Christ. So let's take a moment and bask in the goodness of God to us by examining just three privileges that come with our adoption: identity, intimacy, and inheritance.

---

1. Lewis, *Mere Christianity*, 178.
2. Murray, *Redemption Accomplished and Applied*, 141.

Identity

Adoption is first a matter of identity, or status. It comes with a name change and a new address: we now belong to God and to His kingdom; we now have a house key to heaven. Before, when we were defined by our sin and guilt, the door read "no admittance." Now that we have been cleansed by the blood of Christ (justified), God's home becomes our home. Before our union with Christ we were "children of wrath" (Eph. 2:3), but now we rejoice in the "manner of love the Father has bestowed on us, that we should be called children of God!" (1 John 3:1).

Indeed, this is a privileged status. There is a fairly common misconception that God is the father of all humankind—something known as the universal father-hood of God. It goes hand in hand with another erroneous doctrine called the universal brotherhood of man. The idea is that since we all share God as our personal father, we are therefore part of one big, happy family. But we do not all share God as our father. We all share God as our creator, but this is far from the same thing. The Bible is clear that God is only the father of those who are in Christ. When we are in Christ, we experience a relationship with God that the world does not understand. After marveling in the love of the Father that makes us children of God, John goes on to say, "Therefore the world does not know us, because it did not know Him" (1 John 3:1). Far from uniting all humanity in familial bonds, our adoption as sons of God gives us an identity that sets us apart from the world.

It is important to understand that although we are recognized as sons of God in Christ, we do not have the same relationship with God as Christ, the Son of God. He alone is the eternally begotten Son of the Father. But that is why the term *adoption* is so important. Augustine says this: "Paul says 'adoption' so that we may clearly understand that the Son of God is unique. For we are the sons of God through his generosity and the condescension of his mercy, whereas he is the Son by nature, sharing in the same divinity with the Father."[3]

In other words, the second person of the Trinity is God's Son by nature; we are God's sons by grace. It is a status conferred on us, not something intrinsic in us. It is a legal declaration. We are brought into the family because Jesus shares His sonship with us. The Greek word for adoption used in the New Testament is *huiothesia*—taken from the words *huios* (son) and *tithēmi* (placing). That means we are placed into God's family as though we were His actual sons. This is extremely good news, for if we don't belong to God as His sons, then we won't belong to Him at all.

Intimacy

We start with the blessing of identity, of adoption as a legal status, but we don't end there. If that was all adoption was—a dead, legal calculus—then it would be better to refer to God as our father-in-law and fellow believers as our brothers- and sisters-in-law.[4] But Scripture says much more than that. God is really our Father and Christians are

3. As quoted in Marcus Peter Johnson, *One with Christ* (Wheaton, Ill.: Crossway, 2013), 160. See also Heidelberg Catechism 33.
4. Johnson, *One with Christ*, 162.

our true siblings, in and through our union to our elder brother Jesus. So don't get the wrong impression: this isn't a cold or formal doctrine. I am talking about a legality that in actuality produces and strengthens a loving relationship. For example, marriage is a blend of both law and love—and contrary to popular opinion in our culture, the law enhances and secures the love. Similarly, that is what biblical covenants were: a mix of law and love in which God's binding stipulations brought His people closer to Him. So too adoption is God's covenanting to give us an identity of "sons"—and with that legal identity before God comes a warm and assuring intimacy with God as well.

Abba

One way to prove this is through a single, tiny word in Aramaic: *abba*. This word is used only three times in Scripture: twice by Paul in parallel passages in Galatians 4 and Romans 8. For example, consider Romans 8:14–16: "For as many as are led by the Spirit of God, these are sons of God. For you did not receive the spirit of bondage again to fear, but you received the Spirit of adoption by whom we cry out, 'Abba, Father.' The Spirit Himself bears witness with our spirit that we are children of God." The Holy Spirit tells us—convinces us—that we belong to God as His sons, and one of the ways the Spirit does that is by enabling us to cry out to God, "Abba!"

Why does Paul use this word? You may have heard that this term is quite familiar, meaning something more like "daddy" than the formal "father." This isn't entirely accurate. It was certainly a term used in the family, especially by younger children, but it still had a ring of respect to it. So that is not the main takeaway from Paul's use of *abba*. Certainly there were Greek words known to Paul that would have conveyed the same meaning, but why does Paul choose this one? He chooses it because it is the language Jesus used. It is the very same cry that Christ gave at one of His darkest and most depressing moments in the garden of Gethsemane. It was at that moment, when faced with the unbearable task of taking on physical torment and divine wrath, that Jesus simply yearned for His Father. Humanly speaking, He longed for help. He needed comfort. And with any and all pretense stripped away, He allows Himself to bare His soul, to reveal His fears, and to cry out, "Abba, Father, all things are possible for You. Take this cup away from Me; nevertheless, not what I will, but what You will" (Mark 14:36).

It is that moment Paul harkens back to. He takes us, his readers, back to that scene and he says, "Look! Do you see that intimacy? Do you see that relationship? It is the kind of relationship in which even the Son of God in His hour of darkness can cry out to His Father and know that He hears Him. That is the very relationship you have to Almighty God!"

This is truly staggering. It should take our breath away. In justification God has taken His throne of judgment and turned it into a mercy seat; in adoption we are welcomed onto His lap. That is the kind of intimate access we have to God—and it is experienced most fully through prayer.

Prayer

Let's consider prayer for a moment. It is no wonder that Paul connects the topic of prayer with his discussion of adoption by the Spirit because the two go together. He goes on to say in Romans 8:26 that "we do not know what we should pray for as we ought, but the Spirit Himself makes intercession for us with groanings which cannot be uttered." The same Spirit who brings us into the family of God teaches us how to speak with God as father—through prayer. Prayer is not first and foremost formal address; it is a familial conversation.

In his excellent book *A Praying Life*, Paul Miller says that we need to understand this principle of prayer if we are ever going to pray with meaning. He says the "heart of prayer" is being able to come before God like little children: dependent, messy, filled with questions and also hopeful anticipation.[5] When the Spirit dwells in you by faith, this is what He is teaching you. He is teaching you how to be a child again. He is teaching you that because you are in Christ you relate to God as a child relates to his or her father. This is what Timothy Keller writes:

> The Spirit gives believers…certainty that their relationship with God does not now depend on their performance as it does in the relationship between an employee and a supervisor. It depends on parental love. The Holy Spirit takes a theological proposition and turns it into an inner confidence and joy. You know that God responds to your cry with the intense

---

5. Paul E. Miller, *A Praying Life* (Colorado Springs: NavPress, 2009), 34–42.

love and care of a parent responding to the cry of
pain of his or her child—because you are in Jesus, the
true Son. You can go to God with the confidence of
receiving that kind of attention and love.[6]

And you can do that at any time! Think of how hard it
must be to get a meeting with the president or some other
high-ranking official. Not only is there an army of secretar-
ies and assistants who guard their schedule, there is literally
an army of armed service personnel trained for the sole
purpose of keeping people out. And yet the young daughter
of this important individual can walk straight past all that
simply because she wants to see her mom or dad. This is
the very same privilege we have as children of God: direct
access to Him whenever we want it. Oh, that we would
want it more! I hope you see that prayer, which we often
view as a chore, is really the greatest gift: God bringing us
into the deepest communion with Him that we could possibly imagine. Prayer is a direct benefit of our adoption.

Discipline
A seemingly less appealing aspect of being adopted by God
is that now we also receive from Him parental discipline
and correction. No one likes going through trials. No one
enjoys hardships. But there is at least this consolation if
you are a Christian: hardships in life are further proof to us
that we truly are children of God. This is what the author
of Hebrews says: "If you endure chastening, God deals with
you as with sons; for what son is there whom a father does

---

6. Timothy Keller, *Prayer* (New York: Dutton, 2014), 71.

not chasten?" (12:7). Discipline is proof of real love because if a father didn't care about his son, he would never take the time and effort to correct him. That is why the next verse says, "But if you are without chastening…then you are illegitimate and not sons."

Don't get me wrong. I'm not saying that every trial is a form of chastening from above. Nor am I saying we need to enjoy discipline. I'm not sure anyone ever enjoys their parents' discipline. But Hebrews does say we have to endure it: to be strong, to persevere, to have fortitude, to not grow discouraged and give up on God. That is often one of our first inclinations when things seem to be going badly: "God doesn't have my best interests at heart. Why should I continue to follow Him?" But on the contrary, God's heavenly chastisement is proof that He truly wants what is best for us. Afflictions "are a sign not of God's neglect but of his fatherly involvement."[7]

It is through the trials you encounter in life that God is preparing you for heaven. Heaven is for those who are glorified, completely free from sin. And that process of removing our sin starts now in what we call *sanctification*. Don't miss that this is an exclusive privilege of adoption. Sanctification is for sons, and only for sons. Paul connects sanctification and adoption in the opening of Ephesians when he writes that "He chose us in Him before the foundation of the world, *that we should be holy and without blame before Him in love, having predestined us to adoption*

---

7. Richard D. Phillips, *Hebrews* (Phillipsburg, N.J.: P&R, 2006), 546.

as sons by Jesus Christ to Himself, according to the good pleasure of His will" (1:4–5).

So now that we have been ushered into God's family by adoption, it is the Spirit's work to make us resemble that family. Or put another way, through union with Christ we have been placed *in* the Son in order to be shaped *like* the Son. As the renowned seventeenth-century Dutch theologian Herman Witsius wrote, "The sons of God by grace have some resemblance to him who is the Son of God by nature."[8] We are being Son-shaped for glory, and that takes the discipline and corrections of rebuking and removing our sin. Does it sting? Yes. Does it mean God loves us and wants what is best for us? Absolutely.

The words of football coach Tom Landry are fitting to help us understand God's work as a corrective father. Landry says, "The job of a coach is to make men do what they don't want to do, in order to be what they've always wanted to be."[9] God may bring us through great discipline, but it is all in the service of granting us our deepest desire: to be near Him and become like Him.

Inheritance

So far we have seen that the blessing of adoption gives us an identity that sets us apart from the world and an intimacy with and access to God as we relate to Him as our Father. But there is one other amazing benefit we have to

---

8. Herman Witsius, *Dissertations on the Lord's Prayer* (Escondido, Calif.: Den Dulk Christian Foundation, 1994), 160.

9. As quoted in Ray Stedman, *Hebrews* (Downers Grove, Ill.: Inter-Varsity, 1992), 141.

touch on still, and that is the inheritance that is ours when we become children of God. Again, looking at Romans 8, we see that Paul connects the ideas of adoption and inheritance: "The Spirit Himself bears witness with our spirit that we are children of God, and if children, then heirs—heirs of God and joint heirs with Christ" (vv. 16–17).

Any time you come across the language of inheritance in the Bible, you are really coming across the biblical concept of adoption. And here is where we need to understand something of the first-century Greco-Roman culture and world in which Paul was writing. Today we tend to think of adoption primarily as being for the benefit of the child. Children are rescued from abortion or an orphanage or some other evil when they are adopted and brought into a loving, nurturing family. But that was hardly the primary purpose of adoption when Paul was writing Romans, Galatians, or Ephesians. When a child was adopted, it wasn't for the sake of the child; it was for the sake of the family. If a family had no son, they had no one to carry on the family line, so what would they do? They would adopt a son. They would bring a stranger in and make him a part of the family for the sole purpose of taking over when the patriarch died. This adopted son would become the heir of the family. He was brought in to rule one day.[10]

And Paul says this is what happens to us. This is why the language of "sons" is used exclusively throughout the New Testament in reference to adoption, as opposed to "sons

---

10. See David Garner, *Sons in the Son: The Riches and Reach of Adoption in Christ* (Phillipsburg, N.J.: P&R, 2016), 35–54.

and daughters." Daughters weren't brought into families for this purpose. Daughters didn't receive the inheritance. People think this way of speaking is at best outdated or at worst sexist and chauvinistic. But it is intentional because Paul is making a point: adoption means inheritance and only sons get the inheritance, yet such is the glory of the gospel that we all—male and female—are called "sons." We are all inheritors.[11] Paul is writing about an inheritance that was completely foreign to his audience. It was an inheritance that the world at that time couldn't even offer.

God doesn't need to bring in anyone to take over the family dynasty, as was necessary for some families in the first century. He has a Son, the eternally begotten second person of the Trinity. And, indeed, the riches of the universe are His possession. He is the heir of all things (Heb. 1:2) because all things were made for Him (Col. 1:16). And yet through union with Christ, we can be rightfully called coheirs (Rom. 8:17). The inheritance of heaven that belongs to the Son of God by right is shared with us by grace as we, through faith, become sons of God. We will rule and reign with Him—for we are sons in Him.

Conclusion

The Bible has no conception of a believer relating to God in any way other than as father, and yet, sadly, so few of us do. We may know it intellectually, we may dutifully say the Lord's Prayer each week whenever we are prompted, and yet we often fail to grasp the import of it all. We love

---

11. See Horton, *Covenant and Salvation*, 245.

Him as our Lord and our Redeemer in Christ, we are awed by His sovereignty, we bow before His justice—but when it comes to approaching Him as a beloved child who will never be turned away, we often balk. And yet God united us to Christ for the very purpose that in Him we too would be sons.

Let this truth challenge the lies that so often crop up as we try to identify ourselves. We may think of ourselves as unloved and alone. Adoption teaches us our true identity is as a beloved child. We may at times consider ourselves to be abandoned outcasts. Adoption teaches us that we *belong*— we are members of a perfect, loving, eternal family. We may define ourselves as worthless, but adoption teaches us that we are a treasured possession. We may feel hopeless and that there is nothing good in store for us. Adoption teaches us that we are heirs of heaven. That is the Christian's true identity.

Friend, with your union to Jesus comes every blessing imaginable, but there is truly nothing more assuring than knowing you have more than a Judge in heaven—more than a Creator or Savior even—you have a Father. Perhaps this is why John Calvin's last will and testament reads, "I have no other defense or refuge than His gratuitous adoption, on which my salvation depends."[12]

---

12. As quoted in David Garner, *Sons in the Son: The Riches and Reach of Adoption in Christ* (Phillipsburg, N.J.: P&R, 2016), 311.

Questions for Further Study

1. Is there a difference between Jesus as the Son of God and you and me as sons of God?

2. What are some of the benefits or blessings of adoption?

3. What does it mean to cry out to God with the words, "Abba, Father"? What does this teach us about Jesus? What does this tell us about prayer?

4. What is the importance of Paul referring to all believers—male and female—as "sons" in Christ?

5. How does being identified as a child of God challenge and transform your life?

6

ONE *in* HIM

There is neither Jew nor Greek, there is neither slave nor free, there is neither male nor female; for you are all one in Christ Jesus. —GALATIANS 3:28

In a 2017 article for *Time* magazine, author Josh Sanburn eulogizes the rise and fall of the American shopping mall. He tells us that by 2022 it is estimated that one out of every four shopping malls will permanently close its doors. Why is this the case? Certainly we aren't consuming any less than we were ten, twenty, or thirty years ago. If anything, we are consuming more than ever before. What is changing, of course, is the way we consume. Everything can be done on our phones or laptops now, without the hassle of driving to the local shopping mall. But what Sanburn laments in his article isn't as much the job loss that this trend has brought and will continue to bring but instead the societal loss. He writes:

> In the 61 years since the first enclosed [mall] opened in suburban Minneapolis, the shopping mall has been where a huge swath of middle-class America went

for far more than shopping. It was the home of first jobs and blind dates, the place for family photos and ear piercings, where goths and grandmothers could somehow walk through the same doors and find something they all liked. Sure, the food was lousy for you and the oceans of parking lots encouraged car-heavy development.... But for better or worse, the mall has been America's public square for the last 60 years. [And] for all its flaws, the mall did manage to bring people together.[1]

Harvard political scientist Robert Putnam made the same observation in his 2000 book on the collapse of American community titled simply (and startlingly) *Bowling Alone*. What used to be one of the nation's most popular team sports in the 1960s and 1970s (10 percent of Americans participated in a bowling league) has given way to lanes occupied by solo players. Putnam argued that this was a telltale sign of decline in American corporate life in general. Other studies show that groups like the Boy Scouts and PTAs are witnessing staggering declines in membership.[2]

Putnam concludes that the decline in social activity is because Americans spend their leisure time in isolating activities like watching TV or surfing the web. Imagine, he was writing this in 2000, seven years before the invention

---

1. Josh Sanburn, "Why the Death of Malls Is about More Than Shopping," *Time*, July 20, 2017, http://time.com/4865957/death-and-life-shopping-mall/.

2. José Niño, "Americans 'Bowling Alone' a Warning for Civil Society," American Institute for Economic Research, April 22, 2018, https://www.aier.org/article/americans-bowling-alone-warning-civil-society.

of the iPhone. America has only become more isolated. Go into a restaurant and just look around: couples will be staring into their devices instead of engaging one another in conversation. Today, we cannot possibly brave public transportation apart from headphones that protect us from interacting with other commuters. The closest we get to socializing is by scanning social media in our beds alone at night. Increasing narcissism and escalating divorce rates all prove that even as the world grows in size, our personal worlds shrink in scope. Most people can't see past their own nose, and residents of downtown Manhattan often live in just as much isolation as someone on a deserted island.

But as we see the world slowly but surely turning in on itself, the church goes a different direction. Or at least it is supposed to. We have witnessed society's sway on the church as well: people go to "church" online or attend a church with thousands of worshipers and know not a single person and are not known by a single person, or even in a small congregation some people come in after the service begins and leave before it is over. But beyond these setbacks—and they are serious setbacks—when the church is truly functioning as the church it offers something that this world so desperately needs: *community*.

We were made for community—it was not good that Adam was alone, so God made a partner for Him (Gen. 2:18). Nineteenth-century Scottish theologian James Bannerman went as far as to say (and rightly so) that "according to the arrangement of God, the Christian is more of a Christian in society than alone, and more in the enjoyment of privileges of a spiritual kind when he shares them with others, than when he possesses them apart."[3]

What Bannerman says is profound: we are lesser Christians apart than we are together. Conversely, we are better Christians together than when we are apart. Why is this? It is because community, or communion, with fellow believers is part of what it means to be saved. It is one of the fundamental realities of being a Christian. As we, by faith, are drawn up and into Christ by the power of His Holy Spirit, we are inseparably united to Him. That is what we've been talking about so far: union with Christ. But, dear Christian, the reality is this: you are not the only one united to Christ. Whoever is in Christ is therefore united to you as well. That is what Scripture tells us: we are all one in Christ. We are one in Christ because we all belong to the one Christ. There is not a separate Jesus for different sects or people groups. Believers of all stripes share everything in common: the Word, the sacraments, prayer, and, most importantly, Jesus and all benefits that flow from Him (Eph. 4:4–6).

As we have been discussing our identity in Christ, it is important that we reflect on this aspect as well. After all, identity is a fairly personal term. No matter what my sin may try to tell me, as a believer the gospel tells me I am chosen and precious, pardoned and forgiven, adopted and loved—but the gospel also tells me that so is everyone else who puts their faith in Christ. We have failed to understand our personal identity in Christ if we have over-

---

3. As quoted in Philip Ryken, ed., *The Communion of Saints: Living in Fellowship with the People of God* (Phillipsburg, N.J.: P&R, 2001), 5.

looked our corporate identity, if we have misunderstood or undervalued what the Apostles' Creed has immortalized as "the communion of saints." So what do we need to know about the communion of saints that we have through union with Christ?

Communion Is Where We Came From

First, communion is where we came from. We were made to commune with one another, as I've already said. The society of Eden before the fall was one in which man perfectly loved God and perfectly loved neighbor. The fall, therefore, caused a rupture in the relationship not only between Creator and creature but also between people. After all, it was the first child of this new creation, Cain, who rose up in anger and killed his own brother—taking no time at all for division to escalate into death. Things only get worse from there, as the Old Testament goes on to describe the further splintering of the human race into a multitude of nations that seem to be constantly at war with one another.

The people of God were not spared from this developing sectarianism. By the first century, it was commonplace for a Jewish man to include in his morning devotions a prayer of thanksgiving that God had not made him a Gentile, a slave, or a woman.[4] In thanking God that he wasn't a Gentile, it was as if the man had completely forgotten God's words in Deuteronomy 7:6–8 that the Hebrews were not chosen because they were any better than the Gentiles.

---

4. See Timothy George, *Galatians*, New American Commentary 30 (Nashville: Broadman & Holman, 1994), 285.

Everyone was equally dignified as part of God's creation, just as everyone was equally defiled because of sin. Israel was chosen purely because of God's love—that didn't make them better than anyone else. In giving thanks that he wasn't a slave, the man seemed to think that the human institution of slavery somehow reflected a divine evaluation of worth. In giving thanks that he was not created a woman, the man was considering the worst possibility yet. Laws and regulations in the secular world, as well as those that had cropped up in Judaism, regarded women as essentially the lowest of society. He prayed as if Eve were not also created by God, as if she were not endowed with the image of her Creator, as if she too were not formed for the purpose of glorifying God in all things.

But this is what that first-century Jewish man had forgotten—where we all came from. He had forgotten that there is only one human race, and that race was created to be a community. Anyone who entertains racism, sexism, classism, elitism, xenophobia, or any other kind of discrimination has forgotten that humanity was made for union and communion with one another. We must remember that an identity we all share—no matter our faith, race, or gender—is that we are all made in the image of God. This fact alone would be an antidote to the harmful bigotry we see in the world around us, as well as the equally divisive identity politics often promoted in response.

Communion Is Where We Are Going

For Christians, communion isn't just where we came from; it is also where we are going. God was not content to let His good creation succumb to the reign of sin, so He has promised to one day start over again with the new heavens and the new earth. Scripture gives us a few pictures of what that will look like, and do you know what you get once you remove sin from the equation? Community!

Heaven is nothing if not a community. It is a community of the saints from ages past, joined now in the Spirit to the saints of ages to come. But for those who are in heaven, their union with one another has come to its fullest and clearest expression—and it is all because of their union with Christ. We hold on to Christ now by faith, but in heaven we will hold on to Him by sight. And when we see Him we shall be made like Him (1 John 3:2)—it is the end goal of union with Christ. But as we are made like Him—perfect in true knowledge, righteousness, and holiness—it is only then that our communion with one another can come to fulfillment. There is no longer any sin to separate us. That is what is happening in heaven: the fellowship of Eden has been reclaimed. More than that, it has become enhanced. With the backdrop of the division on earth overcome, the fellowship in heaven is even sweeter and more beautiful than the fellowship that we momentarily experienced in the garden.

The apostle John receives just a glimpse of this, and the sight is unlike anything he had ever seen: "a great multitude which no one could number, of all nations, tribes, peoples, and tongues, standing before the throne and before the

Lamb, clothed with white robes, with palm branches in their hands, and crying out with a loud voice, saying, 'Salvation belongs to our God who sits on the throne, and to the Lamb!'" (Rev. 7:9–10). Perhaps then—as he took in the scene of myriads from every ethnicity joining in the one worship of the one God—John would have known what so many other learned Jewish people seemed to miss: that this was always God's plan. God's plan was always to have union among His creatures. It was not good enough for just one people group to be saved—the elect needed to represent the entire intricate tapestry of creation.

So maybe John finally understood what was being predicted about Christ in Isaiah 49:6:

> It is too small a thing that You should be My Servant
> To raise up the tribes of Jacob,
> And to restore the preserved ones of Israel;
> I will also give You as a light to the Gentiles,
> That You should be My salvation to the ends of the
>   earth.

Even back in Isaiah God was saying to His creation, "Understand that you are headed for communion with one another. I will send my Messiah to save a remnant from all peoples and bring them back into the perfect fellowship for which humanity was created." This is the grand trajectory and conclusion of redemptive history: it is an ends-of-the-earth salvation that will be fully revealed only at the end of the earth.

So What Does Communion Mean for Us Now?

So if communion is where we came from, and if we know that as Christians communion is where we are headed, what does that mean for us here and now? I would hope that logically it is obvious: it is something we need to experience in the present. We can't do without it. It is what we were made for, and it is what we are being remade for.

It needs to be stressed that the communion of saints, our being one in Christ, is not something we need to create or maintain. It is not something we need to go seeking after to attain for ourselves. It is already ours. It is an objective reality of being in Christ—and that is really important to understand. It is not something we do, but rather something God has done for us once and for all by His Spirit. We are all united now, whether we realize it or not, because we are all in Christ. If you are born in the United States, you don't go to any effort to try to earn your citizenship. It is just an objective reality of being born here. You already are a citizen. Likewise, you don't go around trying to unite yourself to other believers—it is just something that is automatically true of you if you are a Christian because of your union with Christ and our shared bond in the Spirit.

But that doesn't mean union and communion with one another isn't something we should seek to promote and experience. Since it is an objective reality, we should desire a subjective, or personal, experience of it as well.

Purge False Division
We experience that first by ensuring that the church—that is, particular local congregations around the world—is

completely devoid of the divisions we see in the world. Remember that first-century Jewish man and his prayers—praising the Lord that he was not made a Gentile, a slave, or a woman? He had been swayed by divisions and classes the world fabricated that had no place in the eyes of God. And so because of men like this, Paul writes to the Galatian church in Galatians 3:27–28, "For as many of you as were baptized into Christ have put on Christ. There is neither Jew nor Greek, there is neither slave nor free, there is neither male nor female; for you are all one in Christ Jesus."

Scholars agree that this was likely a baptismal formula Paul was quoting, one (or one similar to it) that was used for several centuries in the early church. As believers were baptized, they were receiving the sign of being united to Christ, of putting on Christ, and once Christ is put on He claims those aspects of their identity. It doesn't matter if they are ethnically Jewish or not, or esteemed in society or not, and it doesn't even matter what gender they are because being in Christ supersedes all those designations. Paul is teaching the church that those walls of division that they find in the world are utterly torn down when one joins the church through baptism into Christ—what God has joined together let no man put asunder!

Sadly, it wasn't just the first-century church that struggled with this. Here in America, in the antebellum South, slave owners were brought face-to-face with the disconnect between their theology and their practice. Southern planters knew that baptizing enslaved African Americans would mean they had an equal standing with Anglo-Americans, which undermined the ideology of black inferiority. In response, some planters engineered the doctrine of hereditary heathenism, the idea that African and Native American persons could never really become Christians and so should not be baptized. Others who did baptize enslaved Africans worked hard to reformulate their theology of baptism in ways that would maintain the social disparities of the slave system.[5]

Tragically, while our doctrine might have improved, in many ways practice hasn't. The words of Martin Luther King Jr. in the 1960s in some respects still ring true today: "The most segregated hour in America is eleven o'clock on Sunday morning." The church should be a place where diversity is seen as beautiful. The church should never feel threatening to people of any minority categories. We want to reflect that intricate tapestry of God's saving grace to all people, and shame on us when the world provides more welcoming venues of diversity, inclusivity, and unity than the church. Again, Martin Luther King Jr. is helpful here. He said in a 1965 sermon, "There are no gradations in the image of God. Every man from a treble white to a bass black is significant on God's keyboard, precisely because every man is made in the image of God. One day we will learn that. We will know one day that God made us to live together as brothers and to respect the dignity and worth of every man."[6]

---

5. See Mika Edmondson, "One in Christ Jesus: An Exposition of Galatians 3:28," *Modern Reformation* 26, no. 4 (June 2017): 15–19.

6. Tony Merida, "Martin Luther King Jr., Psalm 146, and the *Imago Dei*," *Tony Merida* (blog), January 21, 2013, http://tonymerida.net/2013/martin-luther-king-jr-psalm-146-and-the-imago-dei/.

Certainly this applies to more than just ethnicity—I am saying that the church must be a place that reflects representatives from every possible category that might divide us. For example, gender can easily separate the Christian community. While factors like age and marital status need to be carefully considered for the sake of propriety, to conclude (as many Christians do) that any and all extra- or nonmarital relationships with the opposite sex are inappropriate is simply unbiblical. We are a community of brothers and sisters, after all, called to love one another, encourage one another, teach one another, and do a whole lot of other things together. Aimee Byrd convincingly calls for the church to recover God-honoring, mutually edifying, opposite-sex friendships—or what she has titled "sacred siblingships."[7] Yet so often we can unwittingly isolate the church into factions through the ministries we put in place:

> Not all men want to camp and white-water raft while drinking craft beer and discussing supralapsarianism. And not all women want to learn how to make centerpieces at the annual spring tea while listening to a light message on a pink passage of Scripture. These stereotypes are not implemented maliciously but are usually intended to serve the congregation well. Still, they contribute to dysfunction in God's household.[8]

The church functions properly when men and women see themselves as siblings, brought together in God's family to advocate for one another and help one another pursue

---

7. Aimee Byrd, *Why Can't We Be Friends* (Phillipsburg, N.J.: P&R, 2018), 145–65.

8. Byrd, *Why Can't We Be Friends*, 40.

holiness. It is part of the way we reflect our elder brother Christ, who is our unremitting advocate.

Age can be another divider that we rarely think about. Senator Ben Sasse from Nebraska decries this in *The Vanishing American Adult*, urging us to "flee age segregation." He explains that because of the rise of the public education system, children spend almost all their time with peers, and with retirement communities the same is true for senior adults. According to a study of Americans sixty and older, only 25 percent of them had discussed anything "important" with anyone under age thirty-six in the previous six months; that number drops to only 6 percent if you exclude relatives. The church should be a place where those statistics are shattered, but the same problem is happening in the Christian community as well.[9] Sasse writes,

> Fifty years ago it was the norm for multiple generations of a family to worship together. But that began to change in the 1980s and 1990s. The rise of megachurches illustrates the ways retail categories have remade our conceptions of community. Just as "mom-and-pop stores" and neighborhood supermarkets evolved into "big-box" anchor stores with demographically targeted specialty shops arrayed around them, mall-like churches now offer services and programming tailored to the market segments inside their congregations: high schoolers, college kids, GenXers, Baby Boomers, and even holdover "liturgical traditionalists."... Worship services are differentiated

---

9. Ben Sasse, *The Vanishing American Adult* (New York: St. Martin's Press, 2017), 89–91.

primarily by musical style and volume—the younger
the crowd, the louder the amplifiers.[10]

An evaluation of churches you often hear from people is
whether or not there are peers for them or for their children. "We liked the music and the preaching, but they didn't
have a youth group for my teens." Don't get me wrong—I
completely see the value of worshiping with people who can
share your stage of life and grow and mature with you. But
when that becomes for us a make-or-break deal in deter-
mining a "good" church, we have missed out on the beauty
and blessing of our unity in Christ with those from a diversity of backgrounds.

Promote True Diversity
That is essentially what Paul is getting at in Romans 12.
He uses the metaphor of a body to explain how there can
be unity in diversity. We all make up different parts of one
body. We have been given a diversity of gifts for the purpose of building up this body, the church:

> For as we have many members in one body, but all
> the members do not have the same function, so we,
> being many, are one body in Christ, and individually
> members of one another. Having then gifts differing
> according to the grace that is given to us, let us use
> them: if prophecy, let us prophesy in proportion to
> our faith; or ministry, let us use it in our minister-
> ing; he who teaches, in teaching; he who exhorts, in
> exhortation; he who gives, with liberality; he who

10. Sasse, *Vanishing American Adult*, 92.

leads, with diligence; he who shows mercy, with cheerfulness. (vv. 4–8)

Where would the church be if it were all young people? How could it function if it were made up of only white-collar professionals? What kind of message would we be preaching if we all came from the same background, social standing, and cultural experiences? We wouldn't be preaching the gospel—that is for sure. Here is what is beautiful about the church: Christ comes to each of us individually and He speaks to us, teaches us, heals us, and helps us in unique ways, but then we come together and can share those experiences with one another. We bring what God has given us, and we give it to the church. We build up the body of believers in ways that only we can.

So as we seek to tear down any walls of division, we do so not by making everything homogeneous and the same.[11] We do so by celebrating our unique and diverse gifts given to us by God. As Mika Edmondson says, being one in Christ is not about erasing *distinctions*, but about erasing *disparities*.[12] It is about claiming our distinctions for Christ and for His body—recognizing we have been brought together to build one another up, thrive off of one another, and live and grow together. The diversity that God has bestowed on us can in no way threaten our fundamental equality in Christ. Philip Ryken is right when he says that "we have the

---

11. As Robert Letham says, "We do not lose our personal individual identities in some universal, generic humanity." *Union with Christ*, 123.

12. Edmondson, "One in Christ Jesus," 17.

best and truest fellowship when we recognize our diversity, but see it as less important than our unity in Christ."[13]

Pursue Frequent Fellowship
This leads to one final, brief exhortation: pursue means of fellowship with the people of God—not just on Sundays (but certainly then, and even *primarily* then—Heb. 10:25) but as often as possible. Through our union with Christ, God has given us this blessed gift of communion with one another—use it! Take advantage of this blessing. It really is a way in which God will bestow His grace on you. How? Because when you commune with the saints, you commune with Christ. Isn't that a wonderful thought? It is true: since believers are united to Christ, He lives in them (Col. 1:27). So when we see a believer, it is God's way of revealing to us something of His Son.

Ponder that for a moment. Let that sit with you. For now, we see the face of Christ in the face of every believer. In their voice we may hear the word of Christ. Thus, in his book *Life Together*, Dietrich Bonhoeffer writes, "God has willed that we should seek and find His living Word in the witness of a brother, in the mouth of man. Therefore, the Christian needs another Christian who speaks God's Word to him. He needs him again and again when he becomes uncertain and discouraged.... The Christ in his own heart is weaker than the Christ in the word of his brother; his own heart is uncertain, his brother's is sure."[14]

---

13. Philip Graham Ryken, *Galatians* (Phillipsburg, N.J.: P&R, 2005), 153.

14. Dietrich Bonhoeffer, *Life Together* (New York: HarperOne, 1954), 23.

Conclusion

We need fellowship; we need communion. It is what we were made for. And in Christ Jesus we are united with an innumerable multitude around the world, down through the ages, and on into eternity. We are given the thing that we need so badly: community—a community that the world cannot give and that you will never find anywhere apart from life in Jesus Christ.

We live in a hostile, divided, and tragically lonely world. Won't you join this community? It is countercultural, to say the least. The identity politics so prevalent in our current culture, while promoted under the guise of unity through diversity, have really just proven to be a means of further dividing our communities. When threatened or hurt, people fall back first to their tribes, then simply deeper into themselves. "If the world is not giving me what I want, then I don't want to have anything to do with the world," so the thinking goes.

But in response to the me-centeredness of today, you can instead be a part of the togetherness of eternity. You can belong to a community that transcends all kinds of political and social barriers. And for those of you who are already a part of it, remember to pursue it and experience it. Do everything you can to promote a tangible reality of this spiritual truth. For we are more Christian together than we ever are apart.

Questions for Further Study

1. In what ways is the concept of community crumbling in our current day, according to both this chapter and your own observations?

2. What does it mean that creation was made and will be remade for community?

3. What false divisions can separate believers from the full communion that God desires?

4. What does Romans 12 teach us about diversity?

5. In what ways is our identity in Christ a corporate or communal reality? Why is this so important to understand?

NEW *in* HIM

For the love of Christ compels us, because we judge thus: that if One died for all, then all died; and He died for all, that those who live should live no longer for themselves, but for Him who died for them and rose again.

Therefore, from now on, we regard no one according to the flesh. Even though we have known Christ according to the flesh, yet now we know Him thus no longer. Therefore, if anyone is in Christ, he is a new creation; old things have passed away; behold, all things have become new.
—2 CORINTHIANS 5:14–17

"Remember who you are." While I was growing up, that was the cautioning instruction from my parents any time I left the house to hang out with friends. The message was clear: I might be leaving the Cruse household, but I'm taking the Cruse name with me. I was to act in such a way that was honoring to my family. With two older siblings who had already earned respectable reputations in our small town, I felt the pressure of what it meant to live up to our family name.

Interestingly, my parents didn't need to spell out the dos and don'ts of right behavior as I went out into the world. There was no "Don't smoke," "Don't do drugs," "Don't break the law" (although for my mom there always was—and still is—"Don't drive fast"). There was no long list because it was all packed into and summed up in that brief exhortation—"Remember who you are"—since being a Cruse already entailed all those things. As a teenager I certainly garnered my fair share of mistakes and parental disappointments, and they could all be traced back to my failure to remember what it meant to be a Cruse.

As Christians, we are meant to do the same thing. As we go out into the world, we need to remember who we are. We need to remember our identity in Christ and live it out. Kevin DeYoung goes as far as to say that the one-sentence summary for Christian ethics is this: Be who you are. He writes,

> That may sound strange, almost heretical, given our culture's emphasis on being true to yourself. But like so many of the worst errors in the world, this one represents a truth powerfully perverted. When people say, "Relax, you were born this way," or "Quit trying to be something you're not and just be the real you," they are stumbling upon something very biblical. God does want you to be the real you. He does want you to be true to yourself. But the "you" he's talking about is the "you" that you are by grace; not by nature.[1]

---

1. Kevin DeYoung, *The Hole in Our Holiness* (Wheaton, Ill.: Crossway, 2012), 100.

Being in Christ Means Being Like Christ

So who are we by grace? What does it mean to be a Christian? We have seen thus far that being a Christian is understood primarily by our union with Christ. As we are brought into this vital union with Him, we receive all His life-giving benefits: we are chosen, forgiven, justified, adopted. This is our true identity in Christ. But if all these things are objectively and factually true about our status as Christians, then it should shape the way we live. Indeed, one of the most important things to understand about being a Christian is that it means—literally—to be a follower of Christ. Or, as C. S. Lewis said, to be a "little Christ."[2] Another way to put it is like this: being *in* Christ consequently entails our being *like* Christ.

New—Now!

The theological term for being like Christ is *sanctification*. Sanctification isn't optional. You can't be a Christian and not become like Christ, or not be sanctified. He is part of our spiritual DNA now (John 15:5; Col. 1:27). We will be made—we are being made—to reflect the image of Christ. Therefore Paul says in Romans 8:29 that those whom God foreknew "He also predestined to be conformed to the image of His Son."

This is what he is saying in 2 Corinthians 5:17 as well: "Therefore, if anyone is in Christ, he is a new creation." This "newness" language is the language of sanctification because at its core sanctification is about eradicating the

---

2. Lewis, *Mere Christianity*, 199.

old ways of sin and bringing us into the newness of God's glory in Christ Jesus. It is about putting off the "old clothes" with all their corruption and filth and putting on the "new clothes" patterned after the purity of Christ (Eph. 4:20–24; Col. 3:8–17). The Christian is one who is already dressed in this new outfit.

Scripture tells this truth numerous other places when it refers to Christians as "saints." *Saint* comes from the Latin word *sanctus*, which means "holy"; therefore, a saint is someone who is holy. "Wait, wait, wait," you may be saying to yourself. "None of us is holy but God alone!" And while without any qualification this objection would be true, notice the way Paul carefully nuances his language when he refers to people as saints. For example, to the Christians in Colossae he writes, "To the saints and faithful brethren *in Christ*" (1:2). Or to the Philippian church he begins his epistle by writing: "To all the saints *in Christ Jesus* who are in Philippi" (Phil. 1:1). We can only rightly be called saints, or rightly be seen as holy, insofar as we are found in Christ, *the* Holy One. This is especially clear at the start of Paul's first letter to Corinth: "To the church of God which is at Corinth, to those *who are sanctified in Christ Jesus*, called to be saints, with all who in every place call on the name of Jesus Christ our Lord" (1 Cor. 1:2).

This is all a helpful reminder that being sanctified (or "holy-fied") is not exclusively a work of the Holy Spirit, which is a common misconception. Paul clearly says we are sanctified in Christ Jesus. But we often tend to view salvation as something Jesus does, and becoming more like Him in our holiness is optionally tacked on to that and accomplished solely by the Spirit. Two misconceptions need correcting. First, sanctification is no more an option to salvation than justification is. Calvin provocatively puts it like this: "It follows that Christ justifies no one whom he does not at the same time sanctify. These benefits are joined as if by a permanent bond.... Now although they may be distinguished, Christ nevertheless contains both of them inseparably. Would we receive righteousness in Christ? We must first possess him. But we cannot possess him without sharing in his sanctification, since he cannot be divided into pieces."[3] According to Calvin, trying to take Christ without becoming like Him is tantamount to dismembering the person of Christ. Salvation and sanctification go together.

Second, while the Holy Spirit is instrumental in bringing about necessary change in our hearts and lives, sanctification is in one sense still first and foremost a work of the Son (as Calvin's comment also attests). It is first and foremost a work of the Son because it is first and foremost about making us like the Son. First Corinthians 1:30 says that God has put us "in Christ Jesus, who became for us wisdom from God—and righteousness and *sanctification* and redemption." Jesus became sanctification for us by coming to live a perfectly holy life, a life entirely consecrated to God and set apart, or sanctified, in all things to His Father. And when we are in Christ we are brought into that—that sanctification becomes our reality by the Spirit of the Son, for the Spirit is always inseparable from the Son. The Spirit is therefore heavily involved in our sanctification

---

3. Calvin, *Institutes*, 3.16.1.

as well as the Son. In fact, the major task the Son appoints to the Spirit is to take the things of Christ Himself and reveal them to us (John 16:14).

This means we are no longer defined by our allegiance to this world of sin—"the domain of darkness"—but by our citizenship in the kingdom of Christ Jesus (Col. 1:13). This is nothing short of the new heavens and the new earth, which is what Paul is getting at when he says to be in Christ is to be "a new creation." Notice the declarative nature of the language: if anyone is in Christ they *are* a new creation. He doesn't say, "If anyone is in Christ, I hope that they would attain newness," or "If anyone is in Christ, someday they may consider themselves new." Rather, if we are in Christ, we are new—*now*. Part of our identity as Christians here and now is that we are the building blocks of that glorious place still to come: "You also, as living stones, are being built up a spiritual house" (1 Peter 2:5).

Driving an Old Car

When I was in seventh grade, I was invited over to my friend Natalie's house to play tennis. Yes, we were playing tennis *at her house*. Natalie's father was a successful anesthesiologist, and her family had the biggest home of anyone in school (two pools, hot tubs, a tennis court—I got lost the first time I was there, you get the idea). When Natalie came out to greet me, I remember being so ashamed of the old clunker my parents were driving to drop me off (a Buick LeSabre that seemed like it was from the 1800s) that I awkwardly tried to come up with an excuse for why we didn't have a nicer vehicle. Natalie, who was hardly influenced by her family's wealth, likely had no idea what I was going on about nor would she have cared either way.

But what my thirteen-year-old self was feeling was acutely indicative of the human condition: we long for the new and groan over the old. We may have moments of gilded nostalgia, certainly. But by and large our money and effort and energy go into making things new, whether that is technology or cosmetology. We are dissatisfied to be stuck with something old, like I was with our used Buick. Even though our society has capitalized on this discontentedness in numerous vain and sinful ways that clearly had influenced me, at its heart it is a good desire. It comes from how God has hardwired us at creation. The fall doesn't sit right with us; we know something is off. We have an innate sense that things aren't working here, that something is broken, and we want it fixed. We were never meant to be at home in the "old" but always to long for the "new" (see Rom. 8:22–23).

As Christians, we get a foretaste of that newness, and we get it in our hearts, which the Spirit has transformed and is transforming. That is our identity as Christians. We are saints no matter how sinful we might feel. We are new no matter how old we might feel. Because we are in Christ, we are going to be like Christ. And knowing that this holiness we are called to is something that Christ has already earned for us and the Spirit will continually apply to us should bring great comfort and relieve much anxiety. What a burden it would be if we had to achieve some kind of sanctity before God in and of our own strength and power! But that is not what it means to be in Christ. As Marcus Peter Johnson reminds us, "We are not called to make ourselves holy; we are called to live out the holiness he is working in us."[4] In essence, we are to remember who we are.

Being Like Christ Means Dying to Sin

Remembering that we belong to Christ and therefore are becoming like Him also means that we are dead to sin. This is what Paul says in Romans 6:1–3: "What shall we say then? Shall we continue in sin that grace may abound? Certainly not! How shall we who died to sin live any longer in it? Or do you not know that as many of us as were baptized into Christ Jesus were baptized into His death?" Notice again the definitive manner in which Paul speaks. He says we *have* died to sin. Not that we need to die to sin, as if it is something that we must accomplish on our own. Our death to sin is a fact of our being united to Christ. His historical death on the cross *for* sin is our spiritual death *to* sin. When He was on earth He had a relationship to sin: He was surrounded by it, He felt its effects, and He even represented it. But now He is dead to it; that phase of His life can never be repeated (Rom. 6:10).

This is the same sentiment expressed in 2 Corinthians 5:14–16. Paul is attempting to drill into our heads the facts:

> For the love of Christ compels us, because we judge thus: that if One died for all, then all died; and He died for all, that those who live should live no longer

---

4. Johnson, *One with Christ*, 133.

for themselves, but for Him who died for them and
rose again.

Therefore, from now on, we regard no one
according to the flesh. Even though we have known
Christ according to the flesh, yet now we know Him
thus no longer.

What is Paul saying? He is saying that there has been a
fundamental change in who we are. Just as Christ has died
to sin and now belongs to the realm of the new creation,
we have died with Him and can no longer be regarded in
terms of the old world.

You're Dead to Me

Many sorry souls have been rebuffed in their attempts to
rekindle a relationship with a spurned loved one by the
condemning remark, "You're dead to me." You can't get
much worse than that. Let's say Tom got caught cheating
on his long-term girlfriend Rachel with her best friend. She
has dumped him, and his world is crumbling to pieces all
around him. With roses in hand he stands out on Rachel's
lawn one night, looking up at her second-floor bedroom,
unabashedly declaring his regret, his sorrow, and, most
importantly, his undying love. And here is the question:
Will she take him back? The window opens and the curt
reply comes back: "You're dead to me!" That shuts down
the conversation, doesn't it?

There is perhaps a no more severe way to express one's
contempt for someone than to tell them it is as if they are
not even alive anymore. And yet that is what we are sup-

posed to be yelling down at sin as it tries to woo us back into a relationship with it. It is dead to us, and we are dead to it. And that is not a feeling; that is a fact of our being united to the Savior who died to sin for us.

Sin as Self-Contradiction

James Montgomery Boice arrives at the heart of the matter when he writes that "the key to a holy life is not our experiences or emotions, however meaningful or intense these may be, but rather our knowledge of what has happened to us."[5] When we fall into sin, we are showing that we have forgotten who we are. For the Christian, sin is an oxymoron—"a self-contradiction in the Christian life."[6] No wonder New Testament writers get so frustrated with us in our sin—because it makes no sense! So Paul says to the Christians in Rome, "Do you not know [i.e., have you already forgotten?] that as many of us as were baptized into Christ Jesus were baptized into His death?" (Rom. 6:3). And to the Corinthians he asks, "Do you not know yourselves, that Jesus Christ is in you?" (2 Cor. 13:5). You can sense his exasperation. Similarly, John makes the humbling and convicting statement that anyone who abides in Christ will not continue in a lifestyle of sinning (1 John 3:6, 9). Marcus Peter Johnson is absolutely correct when he says that "we do more than transgress the law in our sin; we transgress the reality of our existence in Christ. We 'de-create' what God has created and is creating."[7]

---

5. Boice, *Reign of Grace (Romans 5–8)*, 658.

6. Johnson, *One with Christ*, 138.

7. Johnson, *One with Christ*, 138.

So the Christian life entails being like Christ, and being like Christ means being dead to sin. It means recognizing, remembering, understanding, and believing that we already are dead to sin through Him. All the discipline and asceticism in the world can never stop us from crawling back to sin. Only a Spirit-wrought, deep-seated, and full-hearted faith that we are already dead to sin will keep us from it. So we manifest our identity to the world by abstaining from every form of wickedness. We live out our reality by putting the sin that still clings to us to death. We kill it lest it kill us, as John Owen has famously warned us.

Dying to Sin Means Living to Righteousness

But then there is another aspect of being like Christ. For if we die to sin, we can't stop there. Scripture tells us that we must then live to something; we must live to righteousness. So Paul speaks not only of Christ's death to sin but also of His being raised again for our holy living: "We were buried with Him through baptism into death, that just as Christ was raised from the dead by the glory of the Father, even so we also should walk in newness of life" (Rom. 6:4).

Now that we are in Christ, we are to walk, or live, "in newness of life." Or, to use the language of 2 Corinthians 5:17, we are now to live in light of our residence in the new creation realm of Jesus Christ. The old has been put away—put to death—and now we are marked by newness. Sanctification, therefore, is not only claiming our utter rescue and separation from the world of sin but also claiming our citizenship now in the new creation kingdom. Christ has been raised now to the glory, life, power, and newness that are in the heavenly places, and we are to live as though we are there too — *because we are.* "If then you were raised with Christ, seek those things which are above, where Christ is, sitting at the right hand of God. Set your mind on things above, not on things on the earth. For you died, and your life is hidden with Christ in God" (Col. 3:1–3).

This should radically transform the way we think about sanctification. Sanctification isn't about being a Goody Two-Shoes. Sanctification isn't simply being good; it is being like Christ. It is about reflecting the image of God by being conformed to the likeness of His Son. It is about recognizing who we already are in Jesus Christ.

What a sad thing that so many of us reduce the Christian life to mere moralism. We make it about being nice, polite, sacrificial in our own strength — as if that could ever please God or save us. Simply put, God is never going to be won over by our morality or our virtue. According to Scripture, we aren't even able to make morally upright decisions by ourselves, so of course He is not going to be impressed by our attempts to be good. That is why God is far more interested in His Son's goodness than in ours. It is His Son's morality and virtue that please Him and save us. And God is supremely interested in seeing His Son's morality, virtue, and goodness at work in our lives.

So think about that as you set out, perhaps for the first or umpteenth time, on the Christian life: don't try to please God by being good in your own strength; please God by being like His Son. And there is a distinction. Being good in our strength is about us. Being like Jesus is about Him.

Being good through our own efforts can never cause us to be conformed to the image of Christ, but being conformed to the image of Christ will always produce goodness in our lives. When we find our identities in Christ, then our pursuit of holiness will be preeminently a pursuit of Jesus—a way of experiencing Him and our union with Him in more vital and tangible ways.[8] Again, Marcus Peter Johnson is profoundly insightful:

> Sanctification is not, at bottom, a matter of psychology, physiology, or sociology (although it may involve any or all of these); it is a matter of christology. To put it another way, sanctification is not a matter of constructing ethical systems for the improvement of us or society; it is our participation in the holiness of Jesus Christ, who is the "exact imprint" of God's nature. God is re-making us into his image, and he is doing so by uniting us to the One who is that image. Our sanctification is too precious, and sin is far too serious, to be hijacked by superficial notions of morality.[9]

Conclusion

Nineteenth-century Danish philosopher Soren Kierkegaard once told a parable of the church that went something like this:

> A certain flock of geese lived together in a barnyard with high walls around it. Because the corn was good and the barnyard was secure, these geese would never take a risk. One day a philosopher goose came

---

8. See DeYoung, *Hole in Our Holiness*, 98.
9. Johnson, *One with Christ*, 135–36.

among them. He was a very good philosopher and every week they listened quietly and attentively to his learned discourses. "My fellow travelers on the way of life," he would say, "can you seriously imagine that this barnyard, with great high walls around it, is all there is to existence?

"I tell you, there is another and a greater world outside, a world of which we are only dimly aware. Our forefathers knew of this outside world. For did they not stretch their wings and fly across the trackless wastes of desert and ocean, of green valley and wooded hill? But alas, here we remain in this barnyard, our wings folded and tucked into our sides, as we are content to puddle in the mud, never lifting our eyes to the heavens which should be our home."

The geese thought this was very fine lecturing. "How poetical," they thought. "How profoundly existential! What a flawless summary of the mystery of existence!" Often the philosopher spoke of the advantages of flight, calling on the geese to be what they were. After all, they had wings, he pointed out. What were wings for, but to fly with? Often he reflected on the beauty and the wonder of life outside the barnyard, and the freedom of the skies.

And every week the geese were uplifted, inspired, moved by the philosopher's message. They hung on his every word. They devoted hours, weeks, months to a thoroughgoing analysis and critical evaluation of his doctrines. They produced learned treatises on the ethical and spiritual implications of flight. All this they

did. But one thing they never did. They did not fly!
For the corn was good, and the barnyard was secure![10]

I hope it is obvious in what ways the story corresponds
to the Christian life. Why do we often fail to live out our
reality in Christ? Why do we so rarely remember and manifest our identity in Jesus? Because we believe the false
"identity gospel" that says we can be happy just the way we
are, even in our sin and far from God. And this proves we
are too comfortable here.

But this world belongs to the old that is passing away—
just like that delicious corn and the secure barnyard. It
might seem like it offers us so much, but it all has an expi-
ration date. It won't be here for long. It is passing away, yet
we are not. We belong to a new place entirely: a new creation that is begun in us through the reign of Christ by His
Spirit. We belong to that place that is newer, that is better,
that is higher.

So, Christian, live, for you are new in Christ. Leave sin,
for you are a saint. Fly, for you belong to heaven. And above
all, as you go out into the world, *remember who you are.*

10. As quoted in Athol Gill, *The Fringes of Freedom: Following Jesus,
Living Together, Working for Justice* (Homebush West, New South Wales,
Australia: Lancer Books, 1990), 30.

Questions for Further Study

1. What does it mean that God wants us to be true to who we are by grace, not who we are by nature?

2. In what ways is sanctification a work of the Son? In what ways is sanctification a work of the Holy Spirit?

3. What things in life cause you to desire newness?

4. What does it mean to be dead to sin?

5. How can we "live to righteousness"?

8

SECURE *in* HIM

What then shall we say to these things? If God is for us, who can be against us? He who did not spare His own Son, but delivered Him up for us all, how shall He not with Him also freely give us all things? Who shall bring a charge against God's elect? It is God who justifies. Who is he who condemns? It is Christ who died, and furthermore is also risen, who is even at the right hand of God, who also makes intercession for us. Who shall separate us from the love of Christ? Shall tribulation, or distress, or persecution, or famine, or nakedness, or peril, or sword? As it is written:

For Your sake we are killed all day long;
We are accounted as sheep for the slaughter.

Yet in all these things we are more than conquerors through Him who loved us. For I am persuaded that neither death nor life, nor angels nor principalities nor powers, nor things present nor things to come, nor height nor depth, nor any other created thing, shall be able to separate us from the love of God which is in Christ Jesus our Lord. —ROMANS 8:31–39

J. R. R. Tolkien's epic masterpiece *The Lord of the Rings* chronicles the conflict between good and evil in the battle for control of the One Ring. The dark forces of Sauron want to possess the Ring for power; others seek its destruction in order to maintain peace in Middle Earth. As the ranks of Sauron's Orcs and other wickedness grow and spread, the good king Theoden is forced to move his people to the stronghold known as Helm's Deep as a final attempt to stave off the enemy's progress and preserve their lives. Theoden is confident that this fortress, with its high walls and strategic position in the Westfold Vale gorge and along the rock face, is practically impenetrable. Upon hearing that over ten thousand strong are marching toward them, he declares with unflinching boldness, "Let them come." He was certain they couldn't be touched. He was mistaken.

Far from the weeks-long onslaught that Theoden and the warriors of Rohan expected would wear out and deplete the advancing army, the force of the attack and the sheer number of attackers proved too great for Helm's Deep. The wall was breached in no time at all. Wide-eyed and dismayed, Theoden comments to Aragorn, "It is said that [Helm's Deep] has never fallen to assault, but now my heart is doubtful. The world changes, and all that once was strong now proves unsure. How shall any tower withstand such numbers and reckless hate?"[1]

We don't need to reach into fantasy and fiction to find this sentiment. There are countless instances where a trusted

---

1. J. R. R. Tolkien, *The Two Towers* (New York: Houghton Mifflin, 1954), 526–27.

security ended up failing an overly confident people. For the Royal Mail service, size and steel betrayed the danger of Northern Atlantic icebergs, costing fifteen hundred lives in the sinking of *RMS Titanic* in 1912. For France it was the Ardennes Forest, a natural defense so thick and rough that Allied generals were certain German troops would never attempt to cross over it with their tanks. The Allies put all their efforts into guarding other areas of the border and felt secure with the woods to the north. Yet Germany cut straight through the forest with ease in their Panzer tanks, eventually capturing Belgium, Luxembourg, and France.

The security crisis can be personal too. If we put our confidence or identity or purpose into something that ends up giving way, where does that leave us? For individuals who find their life's satisfaction in work, what happens when they get laid off? Or imagine a person whose whole life is wrapped up in being a spouse—how could you possibly comfort them the day they receive divorce papers? Or the professional athlete after a paralyzing injury? What of the perfectionist who has just received his or her first C in school? In all these situations, it is not an exaggeration to say that their worlds have collapsed. This tragic (but true) headline proves the point: "Over Twenty Indian Students Commit Suicide after Inaccurate University Admission Results."[2] Thinking they had failed their entrance exams, these poor students were asking themselves the questions, "Who am I? What is the point of life anymore? Can I ever

2. https://www.telegraph.co.uk/news/2019/04/30/twenty-indian -students-commit-suicide-inaccurate-university/.

find happiness or satisfaction again?" They answered in the wrong way.

But to some extent, this is the existential crisis many people will face at some point or another in their life. Is there any way to avoid it? Is there any solution to overcome it? There is! And the solution is to root your identity in something that will never change. That narrows down the list quite a bit, doesn't it? Jobs change, interests and hobbies change, relationships and emotions will wax and wane, towers will fall, and fortresses will fail. As Theoden says, "The world changes, and all that once was strong now proves unsure."

But Jesus doesn't change—"Jesus Christ is the same yesterday, today, and forever" (Heb. 13:8). And that means if we are in Him, if we find Him to be the all-controlling and definitive aspect of who we are, then we can have security. We can have stability. And we can know that no matter what may come in this life, we will never lose our identity. It, too, will be the same yesterday, today, and forever.

What Are We Secure From?

With Christ comes true security. The question then is, Security from what? We are kept secure from ever falling away or losing the salvation that has been granted to us in Christ. There are three areas in particular that pose a serious but ultimately ineffective threat to the Christian: the world, the flesh, and the devil.

The Delusion of the World

First, we are kept safe and secure from the world. The world is trying to sell us the lie that we can be made and kept happy with things—"stuff"—here and now. Capitalism thrives on people literally buying into the notion that more things will make them happy. Pornography is a booming industry that finds its success in people's misconception that illegitimate sex brings lasting satisfaction. The late Neil Postman famously alerted us to the fact—yet never affecting a solution—that we all are amusing ourselves to death, and for that Hollywood is grateful. Postman's observation in the 1980s is just as relevant today.

But it is all delusion. It is false advertising. None of it will last. None of it will offer the thing we are trying to get from it. Robert Frost captures well the fleeting and illusory satisfaction of this world in his poem "Nothing Gold Can Stay":

> Nature's first green is gold,
> Her hardest hue to hold.
> Her early leaf's a flower;
> But only so an hour.

Yes, though nature's first green may seem gold, the truth is that nothing gold can stay. It can't last. And yet the world will continue to clamor for our attention, yearning for us to buy into their agenda and find pleasure in fading gold. They truly will stop at nothing to win us over. But we take these assuring words from Jesus Christ to heart: "I have overcome the world" (John 16:33).

How has He overcome the world? Jesus has endured the temptation of the world for us. Matthew's account of Jesus's temptation in the desert is a perfect display of this. Satan appears and tempts the Lord three times. Each time is an instance of the devil trying to get Jesus to find fulfillment in a commodity of this fallen world: sensual pleasure, thrill-seeking, and power. But Jesus resolutely declares, "Away with you, Satan! For it is written, 'You shall worship the LORD your God, and Him only you shall serve'" (4:10). To every offer of fleeting happiness He remained steadfast in the satisfaction that can come from God alone.

Moreover, Jesus has overcome by enduring the trials and tribulations of a world marked by sin (Heb. 12:2). He endured the slander and scorn of a jeering people who were blind to who He really was (1 Peter 2:23). He endured deep heartache and emotional anguish over the painful troubles of life (John 11:33). He endured the rejection of His own family and loved ones and the betrayal of His closest friends (Mark 14:50; John 1:11). Yet none of this defeated Him. He overcame the world, and when we are in Him we have overcome it as well.

We need not fear the cruel betrayal of money, fame, sex, drugs, success, or any other avenue of worldly happiness. We know they all will eventually come up short, revealing that they've been slowly killing us the whole time they were offering us "life." But we are kept secure from all that in Christ. Though we will certainly struggle with temptation and all too frequently stumble, we can be fully certain that those temptations will never overwhelm us. We will never ultimately succumb to the power and pull of sin.

For we have something far greater than the world could ever offer us: when we are in Him we find an identity that will never change, and we come into a joy that is not based on circumstances. Jesus protects us from the delusion of this passing world by preserving us in Him everlastingly. Thus we can sing:

> Fading is the worldling's pleasure,
> All his boasted pomp and show.
> Solid joys and lasting treasure
> None but Zion's children know.[3]

The Deceit of Self

A threat that is even closer to home than the world we live in is the one that lives in us: our own thoughts, desires, and warring passions (James 4:1). But to be in Jesus is to be preserved even from ourselves and all the lies we love to hold on to in the privacy of our own thoughts. We threaten our own identity in at least two major ways.

The first is through an unfounded and unsafe sense of autonomy. The modern culture has indoctrinated us with the conception that we are the captains of our souls and the masters of our fate. Whatever we want we can get. We can wake up one morning and decide we want to be a different gender, and the world has facilitated that kind of self-actualization. College campuses are being ruled by young adults who claim any opinions contrary to their own pose an actual threat to their mental and emotional well-being.

---

3. John Newton, "Glorious Things of Thee Are Spoken" (1779), in the public domain.

Constructive arguments can easily be shut down today by simply pulling the "that-may-be-your-truth-but-it's-not-my-truth" card.

In a 2013 article titled "Losing My Identity," entrepreneur Lorenz Sell chronicles a job loss, a home loss, and a challenging breakup that culminated in him asking the question, Who am I? After years of soul-searching, Sell has come to a new understanding of identity. He writes of his own conclusion, but his is representative of the entire modern culture of expressive individualism:

> True identity is being true to oneself. For me this is cultivating genuine self respect and a willingness to be vulnerable. This makes for a more flexible identity that is based on how I feel about my actions rather than the outcome of my actions. If I feel good then I know my behavior is aligned with values that bring me real happiness. In struggling to find my identity I realized that I create my own identity. This is the most valuable lesson that I have learned. When I let go of the need to define myself, I can choose any definition I want. By accepting that I am not limited by any notion of identity, I liberate myself to just be me. Right here, right now, I am choosing my identity by how I am choosing to spend my time. In this very moment I am creating myself and this is my identity.[4]

"I liberate myself to just be me," he says. "I am creating myself and this is my identity." According to Sell, you do

---

4. Lorenz Sell, "Losing My Identity," *Life* (blog), Huffington Post, August 20, 2013, https://www.huffingtonpost.com/lorenz-sell/self-identity_b_3779389.html.

not create your identity by becoming enslaved to external things like work and family; it is by becoming committed to yourself and your true feelings, wherever that may lead you. So what is the problem? Why is this follow-your-heart philosophy dangerous?

It is dangerous because, as we read in Jeremiah 17:9,

> The heart is deceitful above all things,
> And desperately wicked;
> Who can know it?

Our own selves are deceptive. We will follow a passion that promises fulfillment only to find it leaves us empty and wanting more every time. Furthermore, sin has rendered our moral faculties damaged and defective. If we were to heed Sell's advice and do what makes us happy, that would be no guarantee of a good life. Many of the things that make us happy are wicked and lead straight to hell. Other things, frankly, are simply beyond our power to achieve or obtain or retain.

Moreover, it would be absolutely ridiculous to have ourselves as the north of our own compass, for then we wouldn't go anywhere. We need to look outside and away from ourselves if we are to make any progress, and that is precisely what Christianity offers in Jesus Christ: True North. He gives us a new heart by His Spirit's work in us and leads us toward something we can never find in ourselves: an unshakeable salvation in Him alone.

Autonomy sees the individual as supreme and seeks to satisfy the self at any and all costs. If this is one of the main dangers we pose to ourselves, the second is its opposite: an unfounded and unsafe sense of doubt—the thought that we aren't good enough. That we have messed up too many times for God to love us. Or that He is too busy to be bothered by our insignificant problems. Have we missed out on salvation? Is it too late for us?

These doubts try to poison the spiritual life of a believer. And the doubts themselves may even be reason for consternation: "How could I possibly be a Christian if I have doubts?" Being in Christ doesn't mean we will never again have any doubts, but it does mean that we never again have *reason* to doubt. There is no sin so great that God would turn His back on us. There is no sin so heinous that God would revoke His promise and abandon us to hell. The voice in the back of our heads that tells us we are not good enough has to contend with the voice of God, which speaks boldly and clearly from His word: "There is nothing in all creation that can separate you from Me" (see Rom. 8:38–39).

The Danger of the Devil

Being in Christ is also a refuge from the assaults and attacks of the devil (incidentally, fear and doubt are some of his greatest weapons). It is important to recognize that the devil is not some impersonal force invented to scare children into good behavior. The devil is real, and he is our enemy. He is leading the forces of evil to conquer any and all who belong to Christ. He wants you (Luke 22:31). He is likened to a lion on the prowl for its next victim (1 Peter 5:8). The attacks from the world without and doubts within are all weapons in the devil's arsenal. He is marshaling "angels and principalities and powers" to do his bidding.

But if you are in Christ, the devil can't get to you. He will try, but all his attempts will ultimately fail because nothing can penetrate the fortress that is Jesus Christ. In moments of fear we might forget that the devil has only as much control as God allows him (Job 2:1–6). Furthermore, ever since the cross, he has been defeated and bound (Col. 2:15), and though he pursues us relentlessly, he knows his time is short (Revelation 12). He can hurl all kinds of evil at us. Will we stumble? At times. Will it sting? Likely. But will it stick? No. There is no temporary attack from Satan that could ever outlast the eternal protection that is ours in Christ. "Our union with Christ is indestructible. No cosmic power can touch us."[5]

Understanding this, Martin Luther would welcome taunts from the devil because it gave him an opportunity to exercise faith in his identity in Christ: "When Satan tells me I am a sinner he comforts me immeasurably, since Christ died for sinners." By the Spirit's grace, we too should be able to stand firm against the threats of the spiritual forces of evil. No intensity of attack can breach our mighty fortress in Christ. Theoden's observation was this: "How shall any tower withstand such numbers and reckless hate?" The Christian has an answer to the great craft, power, and cruel hate of Satan:

> The prince of darkness grim,
> We tremble not for him;

---

5. Letham, *Union with Christ*, 134.

His rage we can endure,
For lo, his doom is sure;
One little word shall fell him.[6]

How Are We Made Secure?

We have seen thus far that to be in Christ means to be secure from the threats of the world, our own flesh, and the devil. But now we ask the question, How exactly does this security work? Or, How are we made secure? How is God able to ensure that I will not fall away from Him or from salvation in His Son, and that I will persevere until the end? The Westminster Confession of Faith answers that question:

> This perseverance of the saints depends not upon their own free will, but upon the immutability of the decree of election, flowing from the free and unchangeable love of God the Father; upon the efficacy of the merit and intercession of Jesus Christ, the abiding of the Spirit, and of the seed of God within them, and the nature of the covenant of grace: from all which ariseth also the certainty and infallibility thereof. (17.2)

The Unchangeableness of God

In essence, the first thing the Westminster divines say is that our security is based on the nature of God. He decreed salvation in eternity, which was realized in history through the covenant of grace, and none of that can be changed pre-

---

6. Martin Luther, "A Mighty Fortress Is Our God" (1529), in the public domain.

cisely because God cannot be changed. Scottish theologian John Brown of Haddington said that if the elect were able to lose their salvation, this would be "altogether inconsistent with the perfections of God. For, how can he, who is unchangeable, hate those whom he once loved with an everlasting love?"[7]

We can have confidence and certainty of our status in Christ because we have a God who never changes. His works never fail and are never interrupted or broken. Romans 8:28–30 describes for us "the golden chain" of salvation—described as such because each link, or step, in the chain is unbreakably connected to the others:

> And we know that all things work together for good to those who love God, to those who are the called according to His purpose. For whom He foreknew, He also predestined to be conformed to the image of His Son, that He might be the firstborn among many brethren. Moreover whom He predestined, these He also called; whom He called, these He also justified; and whom He justified, these He also glorified.

In particular, we take comfort that it is God's *love* toward us that doesn't change. It is not as though God elected us to salvation and then realized He was stuck with a bad decision He made. No, He chose us in love, and He preserves in love as well. Paul emphasizes that in the soaring conclusion of Romans 8: "Yet in all these things we are more than conquerors *through Him who loved us*. For I am

---

7. John Brown, *Systematic Theology: A Compendious View of Natural and Revealed Religion* (1817; repr., Grand Rapids: Reformation Heritage Books, 2015), 437.

persuaded that neither death nor life, nor angels nor principalities nor powers, nor things present nor things to come,
nor height nor depth, nor any other created thing, shall be
able to separate us *from the love of God which is in Christ
Jesus our Lord*" (vv. 37–39).

It is the love of God in Christ that is secure. His love is
firmly fixed in and on His perfectly obedient and perfectly
pleasing Son. The love for God the Father toward God the
Son will never change; it is secure. And therefore as we are
brought into the Son, we are kept secure in that love as well.

The Perseverance of the Son

Next, the Westminster divines speak of how our preservation is based on the work of the Son, the "efficacy of the
merit…of Jesus Christ." We could put it like this: we are
preserved in our salvation because the Son persevered in
the accomplishment of our salvation. This is how Jude
refers to Christians when he opens his letter by address-
ing "those who are called, sanctified by God the Father, and
preserved in Jesus Christ" (v. 1).

In John 6:37–39 Jesus says, "All that the Father gives Me
will come to Me, and the one who comes to Me I will by
no means cast out. For I have come down from heaven, not
to do My own will, but the will of Him who sent Me. This
is the will of the Father who sent Me, that of all He has
given Me I should lose nothing, but should raise it up at
the last day." This was Jesus's mission: to unfailingly hold
on to those whom the Father had given Him. Anything
less would mean He was either unable or unwilling. Fortu-

nately, neither is true. Christ came and completely fulfilled His Father's commands.

And thus the reason we can be certain that we will not ultimately fall away is because Christ did not fall away. Being in Him means we are in His steadfastness, His endurance, His accomplishment. His victory over sin is the content of our preservation. Though we will be battered and beaten up by trials and troubles and our failings and sins in this world, Christ has conquered the world and has entered the heavenly places. And as a body does not drown as long as the head is out of the water, so too since we are united to Christ and He, our head, is reigning victorious, we can have full confidence that we will not be defeated. Since He persevered, we will be preserved in Him.

The Abiding Presence of the Spirit
Finally, the Confession says we are preserved in Christ because of the continual "abiding of the Holy Spirit" in our hearts. When Jesus says that He abides in us (John 15:4), this is how: by His Spirit. Jesus is in heaven, and yet we are never separated from Him. The Spirit is our tether to Christ, our "lifeline" as it were. And truly, if it weren't for the Spirit being in us, we would undoubtedly fall away. If our union to Christ depended on our holding on to Him, we would eventually grow weak and let go. Thus, Puritan Thomas Boston writes:

> Were it so that the believer only apprehended Christ, but Christ apprehended not him, we could promise little as to the stability of such a union, it might quickly

be dissolved; but as the believer apprehends Christ by faith, so Christ apprehends him by His Spirit, and none shall pluck him out of His hand. Did the child only keep hold of the nurse, it might at length grow weary, and let go its hold, and so fall away: but if she have her arms about the child, it is in no hazard of falling away, even though it be not actually holding her. So, whatever sinful intermissions may happen in the exercise of faith, yet the union remains sure, by reason of the constant indwelling of the Spirit.[8]

The Holy Spirit is God's down payment, or guarantee to us, that what He is beginning now He will bring to completion. The Spirit is the Father's promise to us that He has hold of us. How much more tightly could He be keeping hold of us when He has made our hearts His very home?

> Let me no more my comfort draw
> from my frail grasp of thee;
> in this alone rejoice with awe,
> thy mighty grasp of me.[9]

Conclusion

So what do you make of Theoden's grim remark that "the world changes, and all that once was strong now proves unsure"? Admittedly, he is fairly accurate. The world *does* change, although it would be better to say that things that once *seemed* strong now prove untrue—because Jesus

---

8. Thomas Boston, *Human Nature in Its Fourfold State* (Edinburgh: Banner of Truth, 1989), 282–83.

9. John Campbell Shairp, "From Noon of Joy to Night of Doubt" (1871), in the public domain.

is strong, and He always will be. Jesus Christ is the same strong Savior yesterday, today, and forever. And that means if we are in Him, if we find Him to be the all-controlling and definitive aspect of who we are, then we can have security. We can have stability. And you can know that no matter what may come in this life, no matter what struggle you may face, no matter what the devil may throw at you, if you are in Christ you can have something that no one and nothing else can offer you: confidence, assurance, safety, and security.

Questions for Further Study

1. What are examples of some false identities you may be tempted to put your security in?

2. How do the world, the flesh, and the devil try to threaten our security in Christ?

3. What do you think of the statement "True identity is being true to oneself"?

4. In what ways are all three persons of the Trinity at work in preserving us?

5. How does the doctrine of the perseverance or preservation of the saints comfort you?

9

ALIVE *in* HIM

In Christ all shall be made alive.
—1 CORINTHIANS 15:22

In *A Brief History of Thought*, renowned French philosopher Luc Ferry makes the claim that the goals of religion and philosophy are the same: to rescue us from death. Mortality is the unavoidable, and humans are the only species that has an awareness of their finitude. Thus the human "cannot prevent himself from thinking about this state of affairs, which is disturbing."[1] Therefore, according to Ferry, "all religions strive, in different ways, to promise us eternal life; to reassure us that one day we will be reunited with our loved ones—parents and friends, brothers and sisters, husbands and wives, children and grandchildren—from whom life on earth must eventually separate us."[2]

This is where philosophy and religion part ways. While philosophy claims to save us, its salvation is not from

1. Luc Ferry, *A Brief History of Thought* (New York: Harper Perennial, 2011), 4.
2. Ferry, *Brief History of Thought*, 5.

death but from the anxiety death causes. This is how a person attains the "good life": by being free from the fear of the inevitable. So Ferry writes, "Unable to bring himself to believe in a God who offers salvation, the philosopher is above all one who believes that by understanding the world, by understanding ourselves and others as far as our intelligence permits, we shall succeed in overcoming fear, through clear-sightedness rather than blind faith."[3]

Ferry, of course, falls into the latter camp. Admittedly, if there is no God, this is the camp to be in because, at least in Ferry's terminology, philosophy is a more sincere and honest approach to the big questions of life. While religion might allay the fears of death, it would ultimately mean living a lie—deluding and distracting yourself with the fantasy of life after death. On the other hand, if Ferry is wrong, then the tables turn. This philosophical approach would be the delusion, and while it might allay the fears of death, it would be of no help at all when death inescapably approaches.

Christianity doesn't present the illusion of life. It doesn't taunt its followers with false hope, like a carrot on a stick. Christianity offers Life itself—with a capital L—Life to the fullest. And it does so only through our union with Jesus Christ, the ever-living Lord. In fact, life is the ultimate blessing of union with Christ. Our attaining and experiencing the full measure of life—what we sometimes call glorification—is the end goal of our being united to Christ.

3. Ferry, *Brief History of Thought*, 6.

As John Murray says, "It is the completion of the whole process of redemption."[4]

I want you to see that. I want you to sense that. I want you to know that in Christ, and only in Christ, are you really and truly alive.

Life at Regeneration

One of the ways we know that God's promise of eternal life isn't a lie, and therefore religion not a fantasy, is because God gives us a taste of that eternal life in the here and now. The first experience Christians have of being alive in Christ, the first genuine hope they are given that death cannot defeat them, is in regeneration. Regeneration, or conversion, is the start of the Christian's eternal life. It is in the name itself, since *regeneration* means "new birth," new life.

"Born Again to a Living Hope"

Scripture speaks of this in multiple places. It is the puzzling instruction Jesus gives to a questioning Nicodemus regarding the kingdom of heaven: "Most assuredly, I say to you, unless one is born again, he cannot see the kingdom of God" (John 3:3). We need to be born again, or born spiritually, because being born naturally is tantamount to death. We are dead in sins and "by nature children of wrath," according to the apostle Paul (Eph. 2:1, 3). This spiritual death that marks us from birth renders us completely

---

4. Murray, *Redemption Accomplished and Applied*, 185.

unable to do anything to change our predicament. You can't tell a dead person to live, after all.

That is why the Christian life starts with regeneration. It doesn't start with us putting our faith in Jesus Christ or with us repenting of our sins. We have faith and repent precisely because we have been brought to life through the power of God, by the regeneration of the Holy Spirit (Titus 3:5). Peter opens his first epistle by launching into a doxology to God for this work: "Blessed be the God and Father of our Lord Jesus Christ, who according to His abundant mercy has begotten us again to a living hope through the resurrection of Jesus Christ from the dead" (1:3). Peter is saying that in God's mercy we have been born again to experience the *living* hope that comes from the resurrection of Jesus Christ. In other words, God brings us to life (regeneration) to experience the hope of life to come (glorification), all guaranteed to us because Jesus lives (resurrection). It is all life! And it is all a work of God. We do not bring ourselves into this glorious estate. Rather, He has *caused* us to be born again to experience and enjoy this life that is ours in Christ.

Notice how Paul, too, emphasizes the work of God in Ephesians 2:4–7: "But God, who is rich in mercy, because of His great love with which He loved us, even when we were dead in trespasses, made us alive together with Christ (by grace you have been saved), and raised us up together, and made us sit together in the heavenly places in Christ Jesus, that in the ages to come He might show the exceeding riches of His grace in His kindness toward us in Christ Jesus."

God has "made us alive together with Christ." We are enabled to experience the life that the very Son of God experiences (see Gal. 2:20)—a life that is full and free and that this world cannot contain. And so we are, spiritually speaking, seated with Christ in the heavenly places even now.

A New, Obedient Heart

This new life, this regenerated self, is referred to elsewhere in Scripture as having a new heart. This makes sense since the heart is in many ways the sum of our personal existence. We need this new, Spirit-filled heart pumping life into us. Again, we must see this as a work that God does for us to bring us to Him, not something we need to do. Ezekiel 36:26–27 is clear that God is the executor of this work: "*I* will give you a new heart and put a new spirit within you; *I* will take the heart of stone out of your flesh and give you a heart of flesh. *I* will put My Spirit within you and *cause* you to walk in My statutes."

When we have this new, Spirit-filled heart, we begin to live in new ways. We are able to walk in the statutes of the Lord and to obey His rules. Sin no longer has dominion over us, and that is a sign that there is life in us. Because sin belongs to the realm of death and decay, any time we choose obedience over sin is proof that we indeed have life. Moses makes the connection between obedience to God's law and life in Deuteronomy 30:15–19 when he preaches to Israel:

See, I have set before you today life and good, death
and evil, in that I command you today to love the
LORD your God, to walk in His ways, and to keep His
commandments, His statutes, and His judgments,
that you may live and multiply; and the LORD your
God will bless you in the land which you go to possess. But if your heart turns away so that you do not
hear, and are drawn away, and worship other gods
and serve them, I announce to you today that you
shall surely perish.... Therefore choose life.

While undoubtedly many religions extend the hope of
life eternal, only the Christian religion gives a down payment of it here and now through the indwelling of the
Holy Spirit in our hearts. His presence is proof to us saying, "Wait, there is more!" That is essentially what Paul says
in Ephesians 2:7: "*in the ages to come* He might show the
exceeding riches of His grace in His kindness toward us in
Christ Jesus." We are alive in Christ now, but we have more
life to experience in the future. One hymn writer captures
it like this:

> God lifted me up to the heavenly realms
> Where seated with Christ I am free.
> In ages to come He will show me more grace:
> So great is His kindness to me.[5]

5. James Montgomery Boice, "Alive in Christ," in *Hymns for a Modern Reformation*, by James Montgomery Boice and Paul Steven Jones
(Philadelphia: Tenth Presbyterian Church, 2000), 25.

Life at Death

So when do we get that greater and richer experience of Life? Paradoxically, it is at death. If God first gives us life through regeneration, He does so second at the death of the believer. It is at death that we enter into everlasting life— into heaven and the presence of God. This is exponentially greater than the life we experience now. Faith becomes sight; prayer turns to praise. Richard Baxter explains the escalation succinctly: "Rebirth brings us into the kingdom of grace; death brings us into the kingdom of glory."[6]

What so many people fear, the Christian can face with boldness and even hopeful anticipation, all because of our union with Christ. Since He defeated death, we will defeat it too. The doctrine of union with Christ is never more practical than when a Christian is lying on his or her deathbed. This is why one Reformed pastor could answer, when asked if he feared the death that was quickly approaching, "No. I shall change my place, but I shall not change my company."[7]

There is no greater explanation or definition of what happens to the believer at the moment of death than the Westminster Shorter Catechism. In question 37 the Catechism asks, "What benefits do believers receive from Christ at death?" Answer: "The souls of believers are at their death made perfect in holiness, and do immediately pass into glory; and their bodies, being still united to Christ, do rest in their graves till the resurrection." This answer tells us of two changes that happen to the believer at death. The

---

6. I. D. E. Thomas, *A Puritan Golden Treasury* (Edinburgh: Banner of Truth, 1977), 70.

7. Attributed to John Preston.

first is that the remnant of sin is completely eradicated, the inward holy warfare against sin is done forever, and the soul is made perfect in holiness. It is completely and totally consecrated to God. All defects are perfected, all impurities made pure. The second change is a consequence of the first. Now that we are entirely holy, without a spot or stain of sin, we can change our location. We can now enter the very presence of God. Hebrews 12:14 says that without holiness "no one will see the Lord." Yet now that we are made holy, we are able to enter into the holy of holies. At death, we come into the presence of almighty God in Christ Jesus.

No Waiting Room in Heaven

And notice how the divines are careful to point out that this happens "immediately." Immediately is something we don't get very often in this life, even though it is something we almost always want. I vividly remember in my second year of seminary waking up in the middle of the night to extreme chest pain. I had never thought I would know what a stroke felt like (or was it a heart attack?) at the age of twenty-four. One thing was clear: I needed help, and I needed it now.

My wife, Kerri Ann, got me into the car and sped off to the emergency room. One problem: the hospital had recently shut down that particular trauma center. We had to turn around and drive to the hospital on the other end of town. We had been living in California for over a year but didn't often make trips to this hospital late at night. We got turned around a few times until Kerri Ann could manage the GPS, all while I was clutching my chest and screaming in pain—not distracting at all for her, I'm sure.

This was my first emergency room visit, and when we arrived I was shocked. Where was the sense of urgency? Why were there no EMTs bursting down the door? Where were the doctors and nurses wheeling gurneys down the hall as they barked orders at each other? We approached the desk, and even while explaining that my heart was exploding before their very eyes, the orderly calmly (and slowly) made me answer about three pages' worth of personal information. Then I was told to take a seat. Yes, I received an EKG shortly after my arrival, but even then it was administered with sloth-like zeal.

It was an hour and a half before I was taken from the waiting room to see a doctor. I couldn't believe it. In my mind, I was at death's door.[8] I needed medical attention *immediately*. In my time of need and crisis, where was the help? Where was the aid? Where was the rescue? It was behind the double doors working on fifteen other people who got there before me. Here I was in the emergency room, and I was being told to wait. They were busy. Along with the pain was a miserable, panic-inducing feeling.

I'm sure you can share a similar story of wanting—even needing—help immediately and instead being forced to wait. You've had to suffer. But will there ever be a moment when we will want immediate aid and immediate comfort more than when we die? I'm speaking of when we actually enter through that threshold, into the unknown. It is some-

---

8. It was heartburn, by the way.

thing that no one can do for us or with us. It is not an event we can be coached through. We have no idea what it will be like. Death is our time of greatest need, our moment of crisis, and where is the help?

The Christian doesn't have to wonder or wait. We pass immediately into the presence of our Savior in glory. He is with us every step of the way. There is no waiting room or agonizing in the unknown.

> Yea, though I walk through the valley of the shadow
>   of death,
> I will fear no evil;
> *For You are with me.* (Ps. 23:4)

The Hope of Heaven

Did you catch that word from the psalmist? Why do we not fear death? Because God is with us. Hear this, dear Christian: even death cannot sever our union with Jesus Christ. He is with us to death, through death, and He greets us instantaneously on the other side. And it really will only be then, as we open our eyes in glory, that we will look down and see that He has been holding our hand the entire time. So Paul says in 2 Corinthians 5:8 that to be absent from the body is to be present with the Lord.

This is the hope of heaven. It is to be with Jesus with no mediation. It is to be right there with Him, face-to-face. How many well-meaning Christians have extended heaven to the unbeliever as a means of wooing them to the gospel, when in reality they are drawing them to the wrong thing! Heaven is not the goal. It is not the end—it is a means to the end. Jesus is the goal and the end. Samuel Rutherford was right to say that if Jesus wasn't in heaven, he would not want to go there. Jesus is the Christian's hope, and at death He is ours to hold on to—immediately.

I have seen billboards and have read tracts and have heard preachers all ask the same question: Where will you be five minutes after you die? It is a thought-provoking question that is meant to tug at the heart of the skeptic. But the question never made much sense to me. Where will you be five minutes after you die? You will be so far into eternity that no one can measure! There aren't even five minutes that go by where you are unaccounted for in the care of Christ. The question is, Where will you be the moment, the instant, the very nanosecond you close your eyes and slip off the mortal coil? For the non-Christian, death will go on. It will never end. Ligon Duncan explains, "What happens after death for those who do not rest and trust in Jesus Christ? They get no Christ, which means no enjoyment, no fellowship, and no love.... It is the most solemn thing possible."[9] But for the Christian, death is our entrance into glory.

At the Second Coming
Can it get better than that? Actually, it can. And it does. (Yes, this is another "Wait, there's more!" moment.) Heaven isn't the full extent of our experience of life. It is not the last stop in salvation. We have said that glorification is the end-all-be-all of being saved, but glorification doesn't take

9. Ligon Duncan, *Fear Not! Death and the Afterlife from a Christian Perspective* (Fearn, Ross-shire, Scotland: Christian Focus, 2008), 39.

place fully when we enter into glory. Glorification is consummated when Jesus returns. So while our life begins now with regeneration and is enlarged and enhanced at death, we see, last, that the fullest expression of life really happens at the second coming.

Becoming What We Behold

God made us to be both physical and spiritual creatures. Contrary to Platonic notions that see matter and the physical as inherently evil, our physicality is part of God's good creation. We are both soul and body. And for us to think that we have reached the culmination of salvation or the highest peak of life when only our souls have been perfected is to think too low of God's grand intentions. This is what John Murray is getting at when he makes this sweeping statement: "Glorification has in view the destruction of death itself. It is to dishonor Christ and to undermine the nature of the Christian hope to substitute the blessedness upon which believers enter at death for the glory that is to be revealed when 'this corruptible will put on incorruption and this mortal will put on immortality.'"[10]

In the catechism question and answer I mentioned earlier we saw two things that change at death: our sinful condition is eradicated and the presence of God becomes our home. But there was also one thing that didn't change, and that is our union to Christ: "[Our] bodies, *being still united to Christ*, do rest in their graves till the resurrection" (emphasis added). I will say it again: even something as

---

10. Murray, *Redemption Accomplished and Applied*, 186.

seemingly destructive and final as death can never sever our union to Christ. That is why Paul refers to the "dead *in Christ*" in 1 Thessalonians 4:16. Even after we have breathed our last, Christ will cling to our cold corpse, promising one day to "transform our lowly body that it may be conformed to His glorious body" (Phil. 3:21). That is complete glorification. That is real life. That is life to its fullest—Life with a capital *L*. And it happens when Jesus comes again. Anything less is not the full measure of hope that the gospel extends to us.

Scripture tells us that at the return of Christ we will be made like Him. We will have put on the imperishable of the new creation. Why? Because He will have returned and manifested who He really is to us. We will see Him, and 1 John 3:2 says "we know that when He is revealed [that is, when He comes again], we shall be like Him, for we shall see Him as He is." We will become what we behold.

The Midas Touch

Furthermore, we know that this is the fullest manifestation of life because it extends beyond those in Christ to the totality of the created order. The entire world, which is imprisoned in sin and death, will be given new life on that day, made into a realm fitting for our glorified bodies. The creation is said to be waiting for us to receive this resurrection life because it knows that when we are restored it will be too. Paul writes in Romans 8:18–22:

> For I consider that the sufferings of this present time
> are not worthy to be compared with the glory which

shall be revealed in us. For the earnest expectation of the creation eagerly waits for the revealing of the sons of God. For the creation was subjected to futility, not willingly, but because of Him who subjected it in hope; because the creation itself also will be delivered from the bondage of corruption into the glorious liberty of the children of God. For we know that the whole creation groans and labors with birth pangs together until now.

The world is yearning for the coming of Christ. It is at His return that all things will be changed. Do you remember the ancient myth of the Phrygian king Midas? The Greek god Dionysius grants him the ability to turn everything he touches into gold. This gives us a tiny glimpse of the power that Christ possesses when He returns. Anything and everything in His presence will be turned not to gold, but to glory. His splendor, majesty, brilliance, and purity are so great that they can't help but sweep everything else along with it, bringing all things into the same glorious condition. This is why the "appearing of our great God and Savior Jesus Christ" is our "blessed hope" (Titus 2:13).

Again, Murray is helpful: "When we think of glorification, then, it is no narrow perspective that we entertain. It is a renewed cosmos, new heavens and new earth, that we must think of as the context of the believers' glory."[11] When you grasp this grand scope of glorification, you will join with the yearning, groaning, and longing of creation for the return of Christ. Your every breath will be cries of, "Come quickly, Lord Jesus! Come quickly, and bring us Life!"

---

11. Murray, *Redemption Accomplished and Applied*, 191.

Conclusion

What are your conceptions of the "good life"? Luc Ferry argues that the good life is about intellectually overcoming our fear of mortality. What do you think? Is that how to enjoy life—by ignoring death? Ferry's approach may grant relief from anxiety, but it doesn't grant life. Only Jesus can do that. Find your life in Him. He offers it to you now by giving you a new heart. Then He promises to bring you through this earthly death into a heavenly paradise. But more than all that, He promises to come again in glory and to bring you with Him.

Glorification, then, is the end goal, the purpose, the destination of all the blessings and promises we have received through our union in Christ. When we are finally glorified and perfected, when the veil is at last lifted, when we see the Son for who He really is, then we will be made into what we are really meant to be. Our true identity in Jesus will become a tangible reality. We will be fully alive for the first time—all because of the life that Christ has and shares with those who are in Him. Paul captures the breathtaking wonder of it all in these words: "When Christ who is our life appears, then [we] also will appear with Him in glory" (Col. 3:4).

Questions for Further Study

1. What is the end goal, or destination, of union with Christ?

2. What is evidence that we have been regenerated?

3. Why should the believer not fear death?

4. What will happen at the return of Christ?

5. Do you have a hopeful anticipation for the return of Christ? Why or why not?

10

COMMUNION *with* HIM

*As you therefore have received Christ Jesus the Lord,
so walk in Him, rooted and built up in Him and established in the faith, as you have been taught, abounding
in it with thanksgiving.*
— COLOSSIANS 2:6–7

Throughout this book we have considered how an identity
in Christ far excels any identity the world might offer us.
When we are in Christ we are chosen, forgiven, accepted as
righteous, adopted into God's family, placed in community,
made new, and kept perfectly secure come what may. Our
blessings in Jesus Christ are so expansive that it can truly
be said that our union began in eternity with election and
will forever continue in eternity with glorification.

What a joy to be a part of this grand work of Christ!
What freedom, too! We are not defined by fading interests,
social constructs, worldly success, or anything else that
offers fleeting satisfactions. Instead, we are defined by the
perfect and permanent righteousness of the unchanging
Son of God. There is nothing we could ever do to earn it.
We do not put ourselves into Christ or unite ourselves to

Him. As we have seen, this is entirely a work begun and sustained by the Holy Spirit.

And yet that doesn't mean there isn't a part for us to play in this whole matter. In Colossians 2:6 the apostle Paul says that "as you therefore have received Christ Jesus the Lord, so walk in Him." That is, while "receiving" Jesus is ultimately passive on our part, "walking" in Him is active. In other words, being engrafted into Christ Jesus is a reality we are meant to live out, pursue, and experience.

Decrying and denouncing the culture around us isn't enough—we need to immerse ourselves in a counterculture. Claiming we don't find our identity in the things of this world is meaningless unless we actively and intentionally find our identity in the things of God. John Brown of Haddington writes, "As union to Christ...is the foundation of the renewing of our state and nature, so the continuance of this union, and the fellowship with Christ dependent on it, are the immediate source of all holiness in habit and practice. Hence we are said to walk in Christ."[1]

So how exactly can we "walk in Him"? How can we ensure we are living in the reality of our union with Christ? How can we be intentional about taking in all the goodness and glory that come with being in Christ? Or to put it yet another way, since we have a union with Jesus Christ, how can we ensure we have communion with Him as well?

The answer is that it has to be through the ways God has established. We sometimes call these the *means of grace*—

---

1. John Brown, *Counsel to Gospel Ministers* (Grand Rapids: Reformation Heritage Books, 2017), 31.

that is, the avenues by which God's grace or blessing comes to us. They are Christ's means of building us up and rooting us firmly within Himself. The Westminster Shorter Catechism asks in question 88, "What are the outward means whereby Christ communicates to us [that is, communes with us] the benefits of redemption?" The answer is, "The outward and ordinary means whereby Christ communicates to us the benefits of redemption are his ordinances, especially the word, sacraments and prayer; all which are made effectual to the elect for salvation." We can easily get caught up in certain so-called Christian disciplines and practices or spiritual exercises as a means of "finding God" or communing more deeply with Him. While these at times may be appropriate and beneficial, it must be emphasized that it is through these simple, unremarkable, ordinary means of grace—word, sacraments, and prayer—that God has promised to show up. Here we know we will find Him. As we adhere to these means, we can know we are communing with Christ, who is consistently confirming and deepening our identity in Him. Let's look at each of these in turn.

Word

We begin to understand how the word of God can deepen our communion with the Son when we remember that Jesus Himself is the Word incarnate. All the truth, majesty, glory, and goodness that we find in the Bible are in Jesus Christ. The Bible is a book by Him and about Him (Luke 24:27).

How properly understanding this would utterly transform the way we approach Bible reading! When we open our Bibles we are not merely reading some ancient historical document. We are not merely reading stories about old nations and dead kings. We are not delving into a how-to manual for life. The Bible is about Jesus, and it is a means of God to cause us to grow in Jesus. Therefore, we need to come to the Scriptures fully expecting that we will encounter Christ and be transformed by His power. No other document has that kind of ability. Of no other person than Jesus Christ can it be said that "He speaks, and list'ning to His voice, new life the dead receive."[2] Because the Bible is the word of God, it is "living and powerful" (Heb. 4:12), and when we read it we are drawn into a living and powerful relationship with the Savior.

Interestingly, the Westminster Shorter Catechism makes a point to say that while Christ communicates Himself through the reading of His word, He "especially" communicates Himself and communes with His people through the preaching of His word (89). Jesus says as much when He prays to the Father for the souls of those who will be united to Him through the preaching of the apostles: "I do not pray for these alone, but also for *those who will believe in Me through their word*; that they all may be one, as You, Father, are in Me, and I in You; *that they also may be one in Us*" (John 17:20–21). Paul says that it was God's plan to use something as foolish as preaching to give us something as glorious as Christ: "It pleased God through the foolish-

---

2. Charles Wesley, "O for a Thousand Tongues to Sing" (1739), in the public domain.

ness of the message preached to save those who believe"
(1 Cor. 1:21).

What do you think about preaching? What do you
think the point of preaching is? The preacher's job isn't to
entertain us with funny anecdotes or give us tips on how to
live our best life now. The preacher's major task is to give us
Jesus. He is to put Christ before the people, clearly portray-
ing and placarding Him as crucified (Gal. 3:1). When this
kind of preaching—real preaching—occurs, it has everything to do with our union and communion with Christ.
For it is in that moment of the preached word, in that
encounter between the listener and the proclaimed and her-
alded Christ crucified, that our identity of Christian is being
stamped on us. We go throughout the week with competing
claims for our affections, with the world telling us a perva-
sive narrative about who we are and what really matters. We
are constantly being fed that false "identity gospel": follow
your dreams, "just do you," pursue your happiness at whatever cost, listen to your heart and you'll be content.

But then we come into corporate worship and we hear
the proclamation of the gospel and are reminded of our
identity in Christ. More than being reminded, through that
living and active word we are being reshaped and remade.
Michael Horton expresses it beautifully:

> Even if we are lifelong Christians, we forget why we
> came to church this Sunday until it all happens again:
> We come in with our shallow scripts that are formed
> out of the clippings in our imaginations from the
> ads and celebrities of the last week, only to be rein-
> troduced to our real script and to find ourselves by

losing ourselves all over again.... These then are the
two grand narratives: "in Adam" and "in Christ." One
is a narrative of pointless rebellion against a good
God and his creation, leading only to frustration and
death; the other is a narrative of redemption and reconciliation, consummated in everlasting life with the
Triune God in a restored cosmos.[3]

When we receive the word by faith, and particularly the
word preached, we are being placed back into that better
narrative. We are being placed into Christ.

Sacraments

Contrary to prevailing notions in mainstream Christianity, the sacraments (baptism and the Lord's Supper) are not
primarily a statement of our dedication to Christ or an act
of our commitment to Him. They are the exact opposite.
Through the sacraments Christ claims us as His own. By
means of water, wine, and bread, Christ is confirming to
us that we do indeed belong to Him. For John Calvin, the
whole point of the sacraments is tied up with the doctrine
of union. Union "is the aspect of the gospel that the sacraments are chiefly designed to present and represent."[4]

Baptism

Accordingly, baptism is rightly considered both a sign and

---

3. Michael Horton, *A Better Way* (Grand Rapids: Baker Books,
2002), 52–53.

4. Keith A. Mathison, *Given for You: Reclaiming Calvin's Doctrine of
the Lord's Supper* (Phillipsburg, N.J.: P&R, 2002), 18.

a seal of our being united to Christ (Westminster Shorter
Catechism 94). Paul makes that point in Romans 6:3–4
when he says the waters of baptism are a symbol that we
are one with Christ in both His death and His resurrection: "Do you not know that as many of us as were baptized
into Christ Jesus were baptized into His death? Therefore
we were buried with Him through baptism into death, that
just as Christ was raised from the dead by the glory of the
Father, even so we also should walk in newness of life."

Baptism is the outward sign of the inward, spiritual
reality that we belong to Christ. Hence, "as many of you as
were baptized into Christ have put on Christ" (Gal. 3:27).
It is God's public declaration that we are united to Christ,
that we are part of His body, the church. That is why the
Westminster Confession of Faith calls baptism a "solemn
admission" into the church because it is the sign that God
has united us to His Son (28.1).

But as I've said, it is more than just a symbol of our
union—it is also a seal (see Rom. 4:11). Through the Spirit's
power working through the word and faith, God uses baptism as a means of keeping His elect. We must therefore see
baptism not merely as a one-time ritual but as an ongoing
means of God's grace. We need to reclaim the language of
the Reformers, who often spoke of "looking back" to their
baptism as a way of strengthening their faith and dispers-
ing their doubts. For Martin Luther, the knowledge of his
baptism was the remedy against the devil's taunts. This is
something we don't consider often today, but, like Luther,
we should look back to our baptism to dispel any and all

spiritual fears: "I am baptized into Christ. I am united to Him. He owns me. Nothing can change that."

Truly, rather than saying, "I was baptized," we should say, "I *am* baptized"; while it happened once, it continually seals us into Christ. So, dear Christian, grow in and into Christ by thinking on your baptism. As you witness others receiving the waters of salvation, remind yourself of the promise God made to you in yours and confirmed in your regeneration: you have received His divine seal, the proof of His ownership and authentication. You have now put on Christ, and nothing can change that.

The Lord's Supper

If baptism is connected with the believer's initial union to Christ, the Lord's Supper is then connected with the believer's ongoing participation in this union. It would be hard to overestimate just how important the Lord's Supper is in terms of our union with Christ. It is in the name after all: comm*union*. While we might primarily think of it as being a communion with the body of believers—and it is that—it is also a communion with Christ. In fact, it would be best to give this "vertical" relationship the priority in the Supper. "For we must first of all be incorporated into Christ," Calvin says, "that we may be united to each other."[5]

It is so easy to construe this sacrament as a time merely to reflect on Christ's death and our commitment to Him in gratitude for His sacrifice. We certainly are called to

---

5. Calvin, *Commentary on the Epistles of Paul the Apostle to the Corinthians*, in *Calvin's Commentaries* (Grand Rapids: Baker, 1981), 20:335.

remember the death of Christ in the Supper (Luke 22:19). But it is so much more than a mere memorial meal. It is an event in which we can see, hear, smell, taste, and touch the reality of our identity in Christ. "Our memories of Christ are no substitute for his living presence," Marcus Johnson writes. "Our recollections of Christ's death, as meaningful and enriching as they are, cannot replace our very participation in the One who was crucified."[6]

The Westminster Shorter Catechism explains that through the bread and the wine we are "by faith, made partakers of his body and blood, with all his benefits, to [our] spiritual nourishment, and growth in grace" (96). Just like baptism, the Lord's Supper isn't merely representing something—it is doing something. We are growing in grace, we are being spiritually nourished, we are partaking (that is "union language," by the way) in the body and blood of Christ.

In the Supper, we should see nothing less than the reversal of the fall. The fall brought separation and alienation between God and man. But in the Supper God invites us back to the table. It is in this sacrament that we are reminded, in a profound way, that our identity is now that of adopted children of God who have a seat at the family table. And at this table Christ repeatedly offers not only a meal but Himself as the life-giving food. What a disservice we do to ourselves if we think the Lord's Supper is merely about remembering Jesus. It is about so much more—it is about meeting with God in Christ Jesus.

---

6. Johnson, *One with Christ*, 240.

As we have seen, "for Calvin the primary benefit of the Lord's Supper is that it strengthens our faith and our union with Christ."[7] He understood it to be a help whereby we are drawn deeper and deeper into fellowship with our Savior. Perhaps a connection we don't often make is that it was this understanding that led Calvin to his famous conviction that we should celebrate the Lord's Supper "very often, and at least once a week."[8]

It makes sense. If the Lord's Supper is only a memorial, it would be best observed infrequently. But if it is more than that, if it is at heart about increasing and strengthening our union to Jesus as the history of Reformed theology has taught, then we ought to observe it often. It is part of walking with Christ. It is part of what it means to be *in Him*. This understanding will challenge you to reconsider viewing the Lord's Supper as optional or insignificant. Rather, frequently and purposefully pursue this God-ordained means of grace to receive Christ and all His benefits.

Prayer

Prayer may possibly be the most overlooked of these three means of grace—and how sad since it is the one we have access to no matter where we are, what time it is, or what we are doing. Yet prayer can seem tedious, boring, a chore, an effort in futility, or all of the above. We Christians often have to drag ourselves kicking and screaming to a time of concerted and intentional prayer, only to get distracted

---

7. Mathison, *Given for You*, 41.
8. Calvin, *Institutes*, 4.17.43.

twenty seconds in! Even public and corporate prayer is disappearing from evangelical churches at an alarming rate, and seemingly the midweek prayer meeting is the least-attended ministry of the church. The problem is not a new one, however. Even centuries ago Puritan Thomas Watson observed that "Christ went more willingly to the cross than we do the throne of grace."[9]

Why is prayer often so difficult for us? Maybe part of the reason is that we don't understand that it is a means of Christ communicating Himself to us. In prayer we are drawn into a deeper communion with the Savior. We deepen our union in the Son through prayer because we are participating in the same activity of the Son. Romans 8:34 tells us that Jesus is the one "who is even at the right hand of God, who also makes intercession for us." Similarly, Hebrews 7:25 says that "He is also able to save to the uttermost those who come to God through Him, since He always lives to make intercession for them."

Prayer is the Son's primary business right now in glory. He stands at the Father's right hand as our advocate, pleading our cause and presenting our needs to the Father. When we pray we join in that great work. Through the Spirit's perfecting power, our prayers are made harmonious with those of the Son. The more we pray, the more our will and words become aligned with His. And as we witness our prayers heard and answered, our faith is strengthened and

---

9. Thomas Watson, *Heaven Taken by Storm: Showing the Holy Violence a Christian Is to Put Forth in the Pursuit of Glory* (Ligonier, Pa.: Soli Deo Gloria, 1992), 11.

our identity further confirmed as being children of God and belonging wholly to Him.

Why do you think we conclude our prayers with "in Jesus's name, amen"? It is not just a sign-off or an "in conclusion" way to wrap things up. We present our prayers to God in the name of Jesus because His is the only name that will get us access to the Father. We are unworthy, sinful, weak, and broken. Yet His is the name above every name (Phil. 2:9), and when we pray we remind ourselves that we are in that name.

Conclusion

By the Spirit's power, our identity in Christ must be experienced, pursued, cultivated, and lived out. God has made a once-for-all declaration that we are in His Son. So what are we going to do about that? We must immerse ourselves in Him. As we have received Him, we must also walk in Him. We must impress on ourselves the reality of this new identity and frequently remind ourselves of the true narrative to which we belong. We need to denounce the false identity gospel that the world preaches to us on a daily basis. We need to reject it even if we hear it coming from the pulpits of our churches (Gal. 1:8). We must quit trying to find worth and value in fleeting pleasures and passing fads. We must put on Christ and live out the identity He has given us.

God has graciously given us the tools to do just that. He has made a path between us and Him. By the reading and preaching of His word, through the sacraments, and in the intimacy of prayer, God has provided means by which Christ can commune with us and we with Him. Diligently attend to these means, my friend. Sit under the weekly proclamation of the word, remember and rejoice in your baptism, be fed at the Table as often as you can, and enter into God's throne room in prayer "without ceasing" (1 Thess. 5:17). For when you immerse yourself in these simple means of grace, you immerse yourself in Christ.

Questions for Further Study

1. What are the means of grace?

2. What is preaching? Why is it so important?

3. How do baptism and the Lord's Supper confirm our identity in Christ?

4. What things can motivate us to a better prayer life?

5. How are you doing at cultivating, experiencing, and living out your identity in Christ?